# The Historic Gardens of Wales

## of Wales

### An Introduction to Parks and Gardens in the History of Wales

*Elisabeth Whittle*

Cadw
WELSH
HISTORIC
MONUMENTS

LONDON: HMSO

Front Cover: *A bird's-eye view of Llannerch, Clwyd:
spectacular Italianate gardens now hidden beneath the
turf (By kind permission of Yale Center for British Art,
Paul Mellon Collection).*
Back Cover: *Plas Brondanw, Gwynedd: as so often in
Wales it is the 'borrowed' scenery that gives numerous
parks and gardens their special 'Welshness' (By courtesy
of The Hotel Portmeirion).*
Title Page: *A bird's-eye view of Hawarden Castle and
Park, Clwyd, by Thomas Badeslade, 1740 (By kind
permission of Clwyd County Record Office).*
Far Right: *Topiary and sundial in the magnificent
gardens at Chirk Castle, Clwyd (National Trust
Photographic Library/Nick Carter).*

© *Cadw: Welsh Historic Monuments*

*First Published 1992*

*ISBN 0 11 701578 4*

*Edited by David M. Robinson and Diane Williams
Design by Tom Morgan*

*Typeset by Afal Typesetting
Printed in UK for HMSO
Dd 291796   4/92   C90   29254*

 **HMSO**

HMSO publications are available from:

**HMSO Publications Centre**
(Mail and telephone orders only)
PO Box 276, London, SW8 5DT
Telephone orders 071-873 9090
General enquiries 071-873 0011
(queuing system in operation for both numbers)

**HMSO bookshops**
49 High Holborn, London, WC1V 6HB
071-873 0011 (counter service only)
258 Broad Street, Birmingham, B1 2HE
021-643 3740
Southey House, 33 Wine Street, Bristol, BS1 2BQ
(0272) 264306
9-21 Princess Street, Manchester, M60 8AS
061-834 7201
80 Chichester Street, Belfast, BT1 4JY
(0232) 238451
71 Lothian Road, Edinburgh, EH3 9AZ
031-228 4181

**HMSO Accredited Agents**
(see Yellow Pages)

*and through good booksellers*

Top: *Detail of the great baroque gates at the main entrance
of Chirk Castle, Clwyd.*

Bottom: *Thomas Pritchard, head gardener at Erddig,
Clwyd, painted in 1830 (National Trust Photographic
Library/John Bethell).*

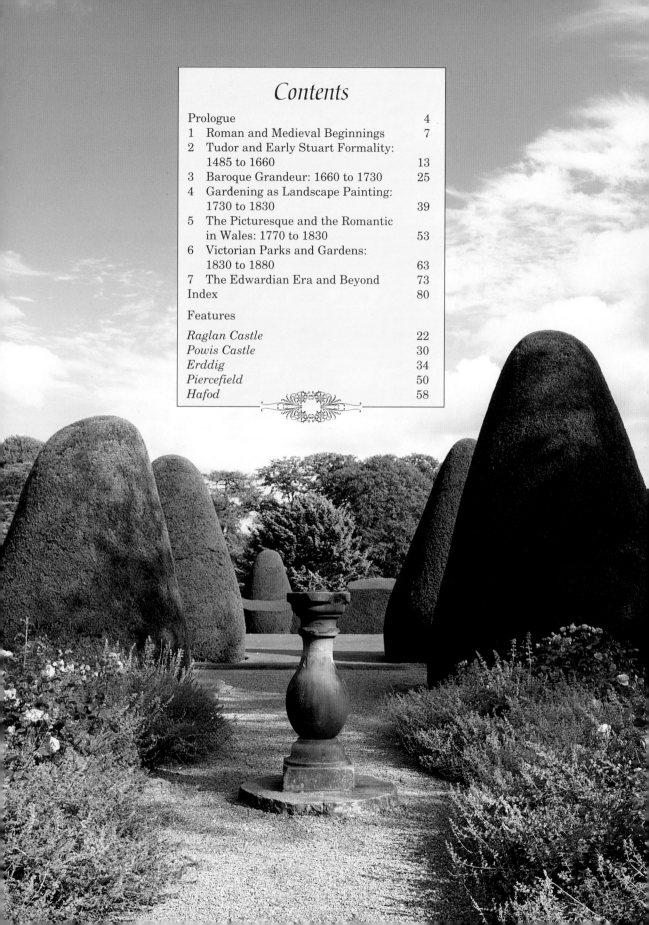

# Contents

# Prologue

**W**ales abounds in notable historic parks and gardens, and in this it is no different from any other region in the British Isles. Wherever people have had sufficient wealth and leisure, pleasure gardens have been the universal accompaniment of habitations. Throughout the Principality, but particularly in the lowland areas, there is extensive evidence for the planting and creation of parks and gardens ever since the Roman period of occupation. As this book demonstrates, very many of these parks and gardens survive - at least in part - to this day. Their remains are an integral and very significant part of the built heritage of Wales. The principal aim of the book is to bring to light this rich inheritance in all its fascinating and wonderful variety, thereby helping us to understand, enjoy and preserve it.

It is important, therefore, to counter the popular misconception that Wales has but few historic parks and gardens, and only a handful that are of outstanding interest. Such a view has been expressed for at least two hundred years. In the late eighteenth century, for example, early tourists saw few flowers; and J. C. Loudon, the prolific garden writer, remarked of Wales in the early nineteenth century, that 'There are no public gardens; but few commercial ones; and the number of gentlemen's seats is very limited'. It may be that the predominantly hilly terrain, together with a damp climate, influenced people's perceptions, and certainly the upland areas of Wales have few parks and gardens. Great was the surprise, then, when the 'highly ornamented territory' of Hafod (p. 58) burst into the view of travellers in the late eighteenth and early nineteenth centuries, 'rising like another paradise, in the midst of a profound desert'.

Parks and gardens were, and remain, an integral part of life in castle strongholds, in palaces and abbeys, mansions and villas, and even at humble farmhouses and cottages. As such, the settings of Welsh homes of all sizes, whether in the form of grand parks and gardens or small enclosures, interlock with the buildings, with the surrounding landscape, and are a tangible expression of the tastes and aspirations of families who owned, and continue to own them. They are just as important in our understanding of the lives of earlier generations as are people's homes.

Why then have parks and gardens been created and tended for so long? What were they used for?

Why did they take certain forms, and why were they altered over time? Why were they maintained for long periods, or sometimes neglected or abandoned? Answers to these questions, even if of necessity partial in places, will add immeasurably to our understanding of the rich built heritage of the country. There is still much to discover, but the story has begun to unfold.

## The Survival of Historic Parks and Gardens in Wales

**A**s one in Cadw's series of volumes exploring various themes in the Welsh built heritage, this book concentrates on the physical remains of parks and gardens. As we shall see, these historic sites survive in almost every state of preservation, for as houses come and go, so too do their surrounding gardens and parks. It might not be immediately apparent to the casual visitor that the earthworks around Raglan Castle were in fact once garden terraces, or that the field below was a lake with an elaborate water garden at one end. The paths of the garden of medieval Lamphey Palace (p. 11) are invisible to the naked eye, but have been found by sub-soil survey, and the fishponds around the site have long since silted up. The layout of a

*The canal and formal garden aligned on the main axis of the house at Erddig, laid out between 1718 and 1733. The gardens represent one of the most significant surviving examples of their period (National Trust Photographic Library/John Bethell).*

garden at Llanfihangel Court (p. 37) is only visible as parch-marks in a dry summer, and the formal gardens of Old Gwernyfed (p. 16), and the great terraced gardens at Llannerch (p. 27), are now reduced to humps and bumps in fields of green pasture. At the other extreme, there are the magnificent terraces still to be seen at Powis Castle (p. 30) and Llangedwyn Hall (p. 37).

Some earthworks, such as Bronze Age cairns or medieval mottes, were occasionally reused as ornamental features in later gardens and parks. But in reverse, garden earthworks can sometimes be mistaken for cairns or mottes. There are many partial remains of features such as terracing, walls, or associated buildings. Indeed, garden and park buildings ranged from the practical to the whimsical, the very small to the very large, the utilitarian to the highly ornamental, and all are represented in Wales. They include summerhouses, belvederes, temples, towers, follies, grottoes, ice-houses, dovecots, lodges and even kennels. Many are ruins, and many have gone, known only from records. Nevertheless, there are some very fine survivals, such as Paxton's Tower (p. 39), the grotto at Talacre (p. 70), the remarkable shell hermitage at Pontypool Park (p. 71) and the eye-catcher folly of Clytha Castle (p. 49).

The gardens at Erddig (p. 34) and Powis Castle

are now two jewels in the crown of the historic heritage of Wales, though both, at various times, have been rescued from near dereliction. Within living memory sheep were munching away at the gardens of Erddig, and in the late eighteenth century the tour writer, John Byng, was commenting on the lamentable state of the park and garden at Powis, neglected in favour of 'driving high phaetons up St James's Street' in London. The owner of the day was only narrowly prevented from converting the glorious garden terraces into a smooth grass slope, according to the taste of the day. In contrast, about the same time, in 1799 the landowner Philip Yorke (1743-1804) proudly opened the first public park in Wales, putting up the following notice at the entrance lodges to Erddig:

*Mr Yorke having at great Expence, and the labour of many Years, finished the Ground and Wood Walks about Erthig, desires to acquaint his Neighbours, that they are extremely welcome to walk in the same for their Health and Amusement; All he requires is, that they will enter and return by the Path across the*

*Meadow, over the Wooden bridge; That they will keep the Graveled paths, and not disturb the Grass or Turf; That they will not pull any of the flowers, or meddle with the Trees or Shrubs...*

# The Welsh Landscape and Preservation

The geographical spread of historic parks and gardens in Wales is understandably uneven. With the exception of Hafod, most are in the more hospitable and fertile lowlands around the coastline and along the eastern Marches. Many do, however, manage to 'borrow' some of the mountain landscape in the distance. It is perhaps this borrowed scenery that gives parks and gardens in the Principality their special 'Welshness', rather than any intrinsic qualities within them. The beauty of the land was drawn into the parks and gardens, and brought by controlled vistas right up to the house. The distant Castell Dinas Brân on its steep hill, and the Trevor Rocks behind, for example, were an important element in the garden of the 'ladies of Llangollen' at Plas Newydd (p. 60). But perhaps the greatest appropriation of landscape is the twentieth-century creation at Clough Williams-Ellis's home, Plas Brondanw (p. 78), where the great peaks of Snowdonia are brought right into the garden.

The care and enthusiasm of owners, whether private, public, the National Trust, or local authorities, are vitally important to the preservation of historic gardens in Wales. Cadw: Welsh Historic Monuments has a somewhat special and guiding role in this work, since historic parks and gardens are an integral part of the Welsh archaeological and architectural heritage. Cadw has in its care many castles, abbeys and houses around which parks and gardens were created and maintained in various periods. Moreover, a *Register of Landscapes, Parks and Gardens of Special Historic Interest in Wales* is currently being compiled under the auspices of Cadw and the International Council on Monuments and Sites. This work is bringing to light a great number and variety of hitherto little known historic gardens. If this book helps to increase our awareness and enjoyment of this rich inheritance, and by so doing to encourage its preservation, then it will have fulfilled its major objective.

*The second terrace of the outstanding Italianate gardens at Powis Castle, ornamented with white-painted lead rustic figures (National Trust Photographic Library / Kevin J. Richardson).*

# Chapter 1
# Roman and Medieval Beginnings

*A sophisticated garden of the late-medieval nobility: detail from a fifteenth-century Flemish illustration (By kind permission of the British Library, Harley Ms. 4425, f. 12v).*

## Before the Normans

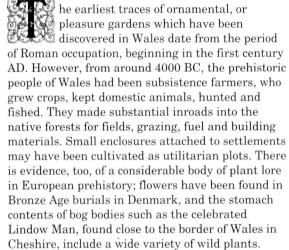

The earliest traces of ornamental, or pleasure gardens which have been discovered in Wales date from the period of Roman occupation, beginning in the first century AD. However, from around 4000 BC, the prehistoric people of Wales had been subsistence farmers, who grew crops, kept domestic animals, hunted and fished. They made substantial inroads into the native forests for fields, grazing, fuel and building materials. Small enclosures attached to settlements may have been cultivated as utilitarian plots. There is evidence, too, of a considerable body of plant lore in European prehistory; flowers have been found in Bronze Age burials in Denmark, and the stomach contents of bog bodies such as the celebrated Lindow Man, found close to the border of Wales in Cheshire, include a wide variety of wild plants.

Following the arrival of the Roman legions in AD 43, archaeological and other evidence suggests that over the next four centuries the lowland landscape of England and Wales was well-ordered, with towns, settlements and farms, linked by a well-maintained road system. Within this framework, sophisticated elements of Roman civilization were grafted on to what remained essentially a rural landscape. Some idea of the extent of this sophistication can be seen in the formal gardens of the palace of Fishbourne in Sussex. In Wales, although the evidence is more scanty, we know that

the legate at the legionary fortress of *Isca* (Caerleon, Gwent) enjoyed a typically Roman enclosed garden-court with a round-ended central pool and a Purbeck marble outdoor dining table. Nearby, courtyards of the large houses in the small town of *Venta Silurum* (Caerwent, Gwent), including one whose foundations can be seen today, were probably laid out as gardens. The large third-century building at the Knap, in Barry (S. Glamorgan), also had an enclosed garden-court, and a villa at Trelydan Hall (Powys) had an ornamental pool.

But this chiefly urbanized style of garden was relatively short-lived, and departed with the legions at the end of the fourth century. The Romans did, however, leave a more lasting legacy. They introduced many trees which later became important both in gardens and in the landscape, including the cherry, medlar, mulberry, fig, walnut, sweet chestnut, holm oak, and possibly the horse chestnut.

There is little evidence for gardens of any sort in the early medieval period, that is in the six centuries before the arrival of the Normans. But a rare and valuable glimpse is provided by the Welsh laws which date from this time. It was in 930 that King Hywel Dda (d. 949/50) called a meeting to approve his codification of Welsh law at Whitland (Dyfed). One of the laws stated that 'Every tree planted for shelter is of twenty-four pence value to its owner, whether planted within a garden, or as shelter to his house'. This tells not of princely

gardens but of the humble utilitarian ones of ordinary people, needing shelter for their homes and food for their families.

*A simple medieval garden illustrated in a calendar for March: a Flemish miniature of about 1490 (By kind permission of the British Library, Additional Ms. 18852, f.3v).*

## Kings, Barons and Bishops: The Medieval Centuries (1066 to 1485)

The evidence for ornamental gardens in Britain increases considerably in the medieval centuries. Such evidence is derived from documentary records, pictures, and surviving physical remains, particularly for gardens of royalty and the nobility. It was at this time that pleasure gardens in which to relax became necessary ingredients in the civilized style of life of kings, barons, bishops and abbots.

There are many pictorial records of such gardens which give a good idea of their general appearance. They were enclosed and inward-looking, often within castle or precinct walls. Their layout was simple, formal and rectilinear, with trelliswork and arbours up which roses and climbers such as vines and honeysuckle were trained. The wealthiest might have ornamental features such as elaborate fountains. The range of plants available was limited to native flora and some introductions from Europe. The most prestigious and heavily symbolic ornamental plants, ones which appear over and over again in medieval garden literature and manuscript illuminations, were the rose and the Madonna lily. But nothing was planted for its beauty alone; everything in the garden had its uses, particularly for cooking, strewing, stilling and medicine.

Orchards were important to the self-sufficient medieval household, and ranged from extensive areas known to have been planted around some abbeys and castles, to perhaps a few trees cultivated by those lower down the social scale. Humbler gardens, too, there undoubtedly were, but we have little knowledge of them. It is reasonable to assume that such gardens were small and utilitarian, with perhaps a few medicinal herbs and ornamental flowers thrown in, rather in the cottage-garden style of today.

## Welsh Medieval Gardens

The early years after the initial advance by Norman knights into the Marches of Wales were a turbulent time, and it seems unlikely that much thought was given to garden-making in lands so recently hard won by conquest. Nevertheless, within decades, there were certainly great deer parks in Wales, and eventually ornamental gardens may well have been established by both native Welsh and conquering Norman alike.

Gruffudd ap Cynan (d. 1137), for example, king of Gwynedd, is said to have planted woods and made orchards and gardens in the early twelfth century. By the late twelfth century the Norman castle at Manorbier had surroundings that were at least appreciated by Gerald of Wales, who was born there. In 1188 he wrote that 'just beneath its walls is a very good fishpond, notable both for its majestic appearance and the depth of its water. On the same side there is likewise a most beautiful orchard, enclosed between the pond and a wooded grove - itself remarkable both for rocky crags and tall hazel trees'.

Although it is known that throughout medieval Europe ornamental gardens were made within and near castles, both by royalty and by those who moved in courtly circles, very few traces of the actual gardens remain. The picture is much the same in Wales, where the walls, banks and ditches of their enclosures and of deer parks, and a few dovecots, wells and fishponds, are all that have survived above ground. Only very occasionally, such as at Lamphey Palace (Dyfed), are there any remains of garden layout. The evidence for medieval gardens in Wales, as elsewhere, comes mainly from documentary sources. Ornamental plantings have long since gone, but a few long-lived oaks and yews remain to tell of deer parks and monastic enclosures. The famous haunted oak at Nannau (Gwynedd) ('Of evil fame was Nannau's antique tree, Yet styled the hollow oak of demonrie'), in which Owain Glyndŵr is said to have dumped the murdered body of his kinsman Howel Sele, survived until struck by lightning in 1813. Yew trees were planted in, or around the edge of medieval or earlier churchyards, and many venerable specimens remain. Those at Overton (Clwyd) are all that survive of the original 21, once hailed as one of the 'Seven Wonders of Wales', and the giant yew in Mamhilad churchyard (Gwent) is thought to pre-date Christianity.

## Great Beasts: Deer Parks

Norman knights were fond of venison, and lost little time after their conquest of the lowland parts of Wales in establishing deer parks. These are the first recorded parks in Wales, fenced or walled and ditched, and stocked with deer. The 'silva de Bruiz', the deer park of William de Braose, at Parc le Breos in Gower (W. Glamorgan), was mentioned in 1230. It enclosed nearly 2,000 acres (809ha), and parts of its boundary bank can still be traced. Many others were established, including one at Williamston Park (Dyfed), the deer park of Carew Castle; one at Senghennydd (Mid Glamorgan), where the boundary bank still exists, and one at Brynkinalt (Clwyd), mentioned in 1399. In a lovely valley on the south-east slope of the Sugar Loaf mountain, Abergavenny Priory (Gwent) had a 600-acre (243ha) deer park surrounded by a bank revetted by a wall, much of which still remains. Some of the buildings of the park gate and park-keeper's lodge also survive. In 1326 the bishop of St Davids had a deer park with '60 great beasts, as well as the wild animals' at Lamphey Palace.

By the sixteenth century many of these parks had fallen into disuse, but several were the precursors of later landscape parks such as at Chirk Castle (Clwyd), Dinefwr (Dyfed) and Nannau. As well as its fallow deer, until the 1970s Dinefwr had a herd of white cattle of a primitive breed, thought to have been there since at least the thirteenth century. Nannau's later park held a particularly small breed of deer, perhaps the descendants of those in the medieval park. The park at Chirk Castle began as a hunting park established by the Mortimer family in the early fourteenth century. Similarly, the park at St Pierre (Gwent), still called the Deer Park, began as the medieval park of the Lewis family; and to the south of Coldbrook House (Gwent; now demolished) was the medieval deer park of the Herberts, which even in 1749 had 'a very good stock of old bucks'.

*Abergavenny Priory had a 600-acre deer park on the flanks of the Sugar Loaf Mountain, Gwent. Traces of the park boundary can still be seen (Photograph: author).*

## The 'Queen's Work': Eleanor of Castile

The late thirteenth-century military strongholds built by King Edward I (1272-1307) in north Wales are the unlikely setting for the royal herber, or enclosed garden, yet this is the next development which can be traced. The creation of such gardens was undoubtedly due to the fact that Edward's first wife, Eleanor of Castile (d. 1290), who spent much of her time on campaign with the king, was an enthusiastic gardener. Within the safety of the castle walls gardens were made for her, first at Rhuddlan (Clwyd) and then at Conwy (Gwynedd). Indeed, accounts of the building works survive, and provide very precise details.

In 1282, at Rhuddlan, the castle well - which had a boarded roof, was surrounded by a small fishpond lined with four cartloads of clay, and seats were set around it. The castle courtyard was laid with 6,000 turves, and the lawn was then edged with staves from discarded casks. Of this ornamental layout all that remains is the well. At Conwy it appears that the east barbican, at the private end of the stronghold, may have been planted as a garden from the outset. In 1283, only two months after work on the castle began, the queen's temporary private quarters, just outside the castle walls, were nearly

Above: *The barbican overlooking the river at Conwy Castle appears to have always been laid out as a royal private garden. It was first mentioned in 1316.*

Right: *King Edward I and Queen Eleanor, from a manuscript illustration. Both king and queen were keen gardeners (By kind permission of the British Library, Cotton Nero Ms. D II, f. 179v).*

Below: *A detail of Conwy Castle in about 1600, from a contemporary painting. The 'litell' garden can be seen in the foreground, in the barbican overlooking the river.*

ready. Here, a lawn was made of turf from the nearby water meadows, edged in the same way as at Rhuddlan. It was given its first watering on a July evening by Roger le Fykeys, one of the queen's squires. The speed with which these ornamental gardens were laid out shows the high priority they were given, despite the primary military function of the castles. At Caernarfon, a lawn was made for the queen in 1283. Two years later, a 'King's Pool' or millpond was made east of the town, and in 1304-05 it was given the charming decorative touch of an artificial swan's nest in the middle. In 1295, after Queen Eleanor's death, the 'King's Garden' was dug and hedged, and by 1343 there was a 'Prince's Garden' on the site of the Norman castle bailey to the east of King Edward's stronghold.

At Conwy Castle, the barbican overlooking the estuary continued in use as a garden long after Edward's reign. In 1531 it is referred to as 'the litell garden', as opposed to 'the gret garden without the castell', which lay just outside the west barbican. In 1538-40, despite the dilapidation of the castle, crab-apples were planted in the garden. A painting of the castle dating to about 1600 shows both the 'litell' and the 'gret' gardens laid out with geometric beds.

There were great noblemen at the court of King Edward I who were also garden-makers of some note in Wales. One such was Roger Bigod III (d. 1306), fifth earl of Norfolk, who had extensive gardens at Hampstead Marshall in Berkshire. In 1270, Earl Roger inherited Chepstow Castle (Gwent), and set about turning the Norman stronghold into a sumptuous nobleman's residence. In a few surviving receiver's accounts for the castle, there are tantalizing hints of a garden feature. 'La Gloriette', close to a gate, is mentioned several times. We have no details of its appearance or precise location, but it was probably a garden pavilion of some sort, and if so it is likely to have been set in a garden within the castle walls.

# *Apples, Leeks, and Cabbages: Developments in the Later Middle Ages*

**A**fter Edward I completed the conquest of Wales at the end of the thirteenth century, more settled and peaceful times ensued. Gradually, this led to the expansion of gardens, orchards and vineyards out from behind castle walls. Inventories of possessions at greater houses sometimes mention gardens, as for instance at Moynes Court (Gwent). An *Inquisition Post Mortem*, a survey carried out on

Right: *An aerial view of the bishop's palace at Lamphey. Beyond the precinct, which was laid out with cross paths, lies the former bishop's park. A detailed survey, made in 1326 records 'sixty gret beasts, as well as the wild animals' in the park.*

Below: *The opening page of the Lamphey entry in the 1326 survey, known as the* Black Book of St Davids. *The survey provides a vivid account of a medieval estate (By kind permission of the British Library, Additional Ms. 34125, f. 30).*

the death of the owner - Bogo de Knovill - in 1307, lists 'A capital messuage with a garden and pigeon house, worth 20 shillings a year'. This document also throws a little light on plants cultivated in the gardens of the lower orders; it states that freehold tenants had to pay one pound of pepper and half-a-pound of cumin in rent to Bogo at Michaelmas. Payment of rent in the spices of pepper and cumin is also mentioned in the Minister's Accounts for the lordship of Monmouth in 1256/57 and 1491/92.

In 1326 a great survey was made of the extensive land-holdings of the bishop of St Davids, one of the wealthiest landowners in medieval south-west Wales. Gardens are mentioned at five places: Trefdyn, Wolf's Castle, Llawhaden, Lamphey, and Llandygwydd, all in Dyfed. At Wolf's Castle and Llandygwydd no mention is made of plants grown, but at the other three apples, leeks, and cabbages are specifically referred to. At Llawhaden two gardens are recorded, but by far the most important and valuable were those at Lamphey. Second only to St Davids itself, by the early fourteenth century the great palace at Lamphey had become a favourite residence of the medieval bishops. It was virtually a country seat, where these powerful prelates spent

more time than at their official residence in the cathedral city.

Lamphey was embellished accordingly to provide a nobleman's lifestyle. The survey stated: 'There are three orchards, the fruit of which with the fruit in the curtilage, in apples, cabbages, leeks, and the other produce, is worth yearly 13s. 4d.; also the herbage is worth yearly 6s. 8d. There are also four vivaries [vineyards], and they are worth yearly according to their true value 5s.'. There were also two watermills, fishponds, a windmill, a dovecot and a deer park. Despite the ruined state of the palace, the spot is still a lovely one, with a great walled enclosure outside which are the remains of large fishponds. An archaeological survey inside the enclosure has shown clearly that the main open area, to the north-west of the palace, was probably a garden, divided into four quadrants by cross paths, whose origins may be medieval. This garden, and even to a certain extent the fishponds outside the walls, would almost certainly have been ornamental. At St Davids itself, ornamental gardens appear to have been made to the south-west of the palace by the great building bishop Henry de Gower (1328-47).

The medieval monastic communities were almost entirely self-sufficient, and can be expected to have had utilitarian gardens, orchards and even vineyards. These would have been within the precincts of the abbeys and priories, or within those of their granges, or outlying farms. Precinct walls survive in part at least at some, for example at Tintern Abbey (Gwent) and at Llanthony Priory (Gwent), which had 12 acres (4.9ha) of orchards and a dovecot. At Valle Crucis Abbey there is a fine fishpond (later altered), and the fifteenth-century bard Guto'r Glyn gave evidence of good husbandry when he said approvingly 'Of Valle Crucis Abbot good, Whose full-stocked tables ever groan'. Little remains of the many monastic granges of the Cistercian abbeys, or those of other orders, but earthworks and ruined buildings at sites such as Monknash (S. Glamorgan), Abbot's Llantwit (S. Glamorgan), and Merthyrgeryn (Gwent), show that within their farm precincts were walled enclosures, fishponds, dovecots and barns. Parallel planting beds are still visible in a small banked enclosure at Bwlch yr Oerfa (Dyfed), possibly a grange of Strata Florida Abbey, and similar, longer beds are visible just outside the secular moated site of Horseland (S. Glamorgan).

## *Peacocks and Figs: Later Medieval Gardens of the Nobility*

Later in the medieval period records give a few tantalizing glimpses of gardens of the Welsh nobility, some undoubtedly ornamental.
A descriptive poem of about 1390, which draws a picture of the Welsh leader Owain Glyndŵr's home at Sycharth, near Oswestry (Powys), by his court poet Iolo Goch, is sufficiently detailed to give a good idea of the motte and bailey castle and its surroundings. The motte was encircled by a moat, and beyond were an orchard, a vineyard, a rabbit warren, a mill, a dovecot, a fishpond, an enclosed pond with pike and fine salmon, and a deer park. Peacocks and beautiful herons are also mentioned, suggesting that as well as a need for self-sufficiency there was also an element of aesthetic appreciation at Sycharth.

There are brief mentions of gardens at several castles during the later Middle Ages. At Cardiff Castle (S. Glamorgan), for example, between 1423 and 1439, Richard Beauchamp, earl of Warwick (d. 1439), added private apartments on the west side of the enclosure, to the south of which was the lord's

'plaisance', or ornamental garden. At nearby Cosmeston Castle (S. Glamorgan) 'a certain garden of the lord with a columbarium in the garden' was recorded in 1433-44. The castle has gone, and all that is left of the garden is a four-sided enclosure surrounded by a low bank or scarp, with the stump of the dovecot in the southern corner.

The most detailed record of actual plants within a medieval garden in Wales comes from an early fifteenth-century document in Welsh about Raglan Castle. This was the home of William ap Thomas (d. 1445), a self-made man and virtual ruler of south-east Wales. At the castle, it says, were 'orchards full of apple trees and plums, and figs, and cherries, and grapes, and French plums, and pears, and nuts, and every fruit that is sweet and delicious'. The 'Blue Knight of Gwent' obviously lived in surroundings of some luxury.

Other later medieval great houses, such as Gwydir, Cors y Gedol, Nannau (all in Gwynedd), Mostyn Hall (Clwyd), and Tretower Court (Powys) can be expected to have had extensive gardens, orchards, and even vineyards. Though few records or traces of them survive, indirect evidence is available in the form of records of hospitality. Welsh bards, ever appreciative of liberal hospitality, recorded the grapes, peaches and French wines with which they were regaled. Guto'r Glyn said that Mostyn Hall 'Has been the hostel of the whole of Wales' in the days of Ieuan Fychan, in the first half of the fifteenth century.

Between the 1450s and his untimely death in 1471, the wealthy Sir Roger Vaughan extensively remodelled and extended Tretower Court, turning it into a substantial and prestigious house. A prominent Yorkist, Sir Roger moved in the mainstream of political life in England, and was widely travelled in the service of Edward IV. It is reasonably certain that such a leading figure in society would have had a pleasure garden for peaceful enjoyment in the quieter moments of his turbulent life. Although there is no direct evidence for a medieval garden at Tretower, the indirect and circumstantial evidence is strong, and a garden such as Sir Roger might have known has recently been recreated on the south side of the court. Its layout and planting are as authentic as is practically possible for a garden of a wealthy commoner in the mid fifteenth century. The tunnel arbour and small pavilion, with vines, roses and honeysuckle growing up them, the enclosed gardens with trellising, fountain, chequerboard pattern of flowerbeds and turf seats, the herbs, irises and lilies, are all well attested elements in western European gardens of the later medieval period.

# Chapter 2
# Tudor and Early Stuart Formality: 1485 to 1660

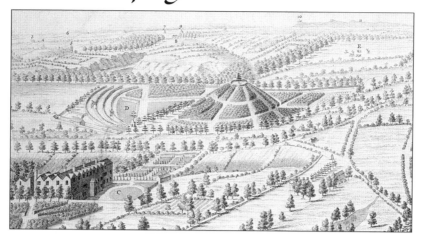

*A detail from Thomas Badeslade's 1735 engraving of 'The West Prospect of Chirk Castle', showing the mid seventeenth-century walled garden with terraces and mount (By courtesy of the National Library of Wales).*

After the turmoil of the Wars of the Roses in the second half of the fifteenth century, and with the Tudor dynasty secure on the throne, the Welsh gentry settled down to a period of unprecedented stability. The Acts of Union in 1536-43 and the Dissolution of the Monasteries between 1536 and 1540 gave them new powers and wealth; the ambitious acquired land, often monastic, and built and embellished their grounds. It has been calculated that there were at least 600 'country seats' in south Wales in the seventeenth century, and north-east Wales saw a similar proliferation. With such country seats went gardens, and in contrast to earlier periods there is far more evidence – both on the ground and in the records – as to what they looked like.

Ornamental gardens of the Tudor and Stuart periods in Britain were both forward and backward looking, with new Renaissance ideas grafted on to essentially medieval layouts. Only the most advanced examples came anywhere near the integrated and axial planning of contemporary Italian and French gardens. Terracing, increased scale, the use of sculpture, and water features such as fountains and formal water gardens arrived in Britain through the medium of the great gardens of France and Italy. The free flow of men and ideas between Wales and the court in London enabled the higher echelons of Welsh society to introduce some of the new ideas into their gardens.

Travel to the continent provided further fashionable elements. In the reign of King Henry VIII (1509-47), two gardeners were sent from Troy House (Gwent) to the continent to learn about the latest fashions and to bring back plants, and in 1611 and 1612 Charles Somerset of Troy visited all the principal gardens of France and Italy. Sir Edward Stradling (1529-1609) of St Donat's Castle (S. Glamorgan) spent some time in Rome, and when he eventually inherited his estate the gardens were embellished, perhaps with ideas inspired from Italy. More settled times meant that gardens could safely extend beyond the confines of walled enclosures near the castle or house, with terraces and pavilions giving views out over the surrounding parks and countryside. In some cases medieval utilitarian features such as fishponds were adapted and incorporated into the ornamental layout. Terracing, walls and ponds have proved the most durable features of these gardens. Raised walks overlooking gardens were popular, and can be found at Tudor houses such as Raglan Castle (Gwent, see p. 22), Treowen (Gwent), and Pencoed Castle (Gwent).

Within the garden all remained formal and geometrical, with square and rectangular plots divided and surrounded by gravel paths, raised terraces and trelliswork. Plants were grown in low clipped intricate interlaced patterns, or 'knots' during the sixteenth century, and later in simpler and more expansive geometric beds, or 'parterres'. The spaces between would be filled with contrasting plants or with inorganic materials such as crushed brick, coal dust, or crushed lime mortar to form a highly coloured pattern.

The range of plants available to the sixteenth-century ornamental gardener was restricted largely to the west European native flora, plus a few exotics introduced from the east and the Americas. Fruit trees were popular and figured prominently in gardens; know-how was sufficiently advanced for exotics such as peaches, apricots and oranges to be grown, and great houses – like their medieval forebears – were often equipped with vineyards.

At the time, instances of this new style of garden layout could be found in gentry houses and castles all over lowland Wales. Sadly, most gardens of the period have long since disappeared, or have been reduced to ruins or earthworks, or in some instances have been overlain with later ones. Most garden plans of the period show a series of enclosures near the house in ad hoc arrangements, with no overall symmetry or axial relationship to the house. Later estate maps, such as the 1738 map of the Mostyn Hall demesne, or the eighteenth-century map of

Llanellen Court (Gwent), show this kind of arrangement, and demonstrate the conservatism of many Welsh landowners at a later period.

At the simplest level, gardens were no more than one or two walled enclosures next to the house. Those at Fferm (Clwyd), a late sixteenth-century substantial farmhouse, are a good example. They are embellished with a simple ornamental arched entrance, and a central path from a door in the house to a gate into the field is clearly visible beneath the turf. Slightly more sophisticated is the terraced garden at the late sixteenth- to early seventeenth-century house of Lower Dyffryn (Gwent), home of a branch of the Cecil family. Here the terrace wall is bowed out in the middle into a semi-circular alcove with seats and a window for looking out across the fishponds (now drained) and the lovely Monnow valley. At Bryn Iorcyn (Clwyd) early seventeenth-century improvements involved encasing the medieval house in stone, and building a lovely series of walled enclosures around the house, one of which incorporates a dovecot. The Tudor Tredegar House (Gwent), according to a tracing of an early seventeenth-century plan, was surrounded on two sides by a series of walled enclosures roughly following the present ones, with

*A section of an eighteenth-century plan of Llanellen House, Gwent, showing the haphazard arrangement of the garden enclosures around the house. The plan shows the survival of garden features common in the Tudor and early Stuart periods (By kind permission of Gwent County Record Office, DA 34.4798).*

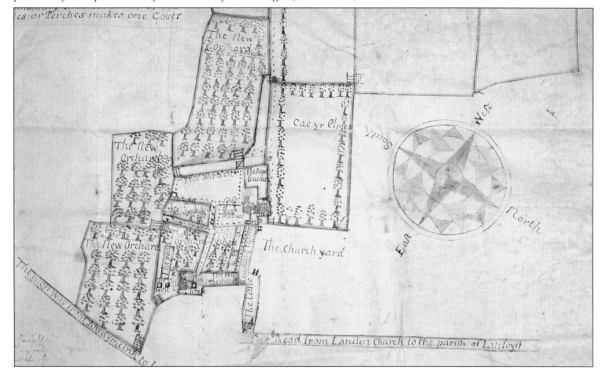

*At Bryn Iorcyn, Clwyd, early seventeenth-century improvements included the construction of these walled garden enclosures with an integral dovecot (Photograph: author).*

*An aerial view of Haroldston, Dyfed, in which the remains of both the house and garden are clearly visible (By courtesy of Dyfed Archaeological Trust).*

a 'great gate' into 'the great bowling greene', a wilderness or maze with a corner arbour, a garden plot 'contrived in walks and borders for trees and flowers' with a 'great walke about', and three orchards with 550 trees planted 'dyamond wise'.

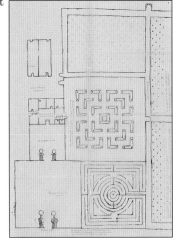

*Octavius Morgan's tracing of an early seventeenth-century plan of Tredegar House showing the arrangement of the Tudor gardens (By permission of the National Library of Wales).*

## 'Old Mansions Fallen into Decay'

Many of the houses of the Tudor and early Stuart periods, and with them their gardens, have either completely disappeared or are abandoned shells. This is especially true of Pembrokeshire (Dyfed). The antiquary Richard Fenton, in his *A Historical Tour Through Pembrokeshire* (London 1803), laments how little notice is taken of 'old mansions fallen into decay within the course of the two last centuries', and gives many examples, including St Brides, which had a walled garden, bowling green and fishponds, 'bearing the marks of having been laid out in walks

between venerable oak trees of large girth. Some of the cowering veterans still remain'. Haroldston was another historic house which he found ruined, and which has now almost completely gone. For 300 years, until about 1700, it was the home of the Perrot family. At the end of the sixteenth century Sir Thomas Perrot introduced pheasants from Ireland, the first to be bred in the county, 'in a pleasante grove of his owne plantinge' at Haroldston. Now only earthworks remain of the extensive enclosed and terraced gardens. Similar erosion has taken place elsewhere in Wales. At The Van (M. Glamorgan), the ruined sixteenth-century home of the Lewis family, the overgrown Tudor walled gardens include a raised terrace walk.

John Panton, MP and recorder of Denbigh started what was to have been a very grand house at New Foxhall (Clwyd) in 1592. Only one wing was built before he went bankrupt, but the gardens were begun. All that remain of them are the walls of the enclosures and traces of shallow terracing in the field to the east. At Old Beaupre (S. Glamorgan), between the early sixteenth and the early seventeenth centuries, Sir Rice Mansel, followed by William and Richard Basset, turned a medieval manor house into an altogether grander affair. Eventually, the house included a storeyed porch, long gallery and other up-to-date features, with a terraced walk beneath the curtain wall, and a garden terrace overlooking the valley to the west, both of which survive. Further paths and terracing are just discernible as faint scarps in the field to the north, showing that the gardens extended out beyond the house to the fishponds next to the stream.

Not far away, tucked into a quiet corner of the Vale of Glamorgan, is Llantrithyd Place, built in the first half of the sixteenth century by a junior branch of the Basset family of Old Beaupre. The Aubrey family, who owned the house from the late sixteenth century, abandoned it in the eighteenth century, and no subsequent alterations were made. Although the house is now a ruin, the structure of its gardens is largely intact. They are thought to have been made in the second half of the sixteenth century by Anthony Mansel, who married into the Basset family. Two walled terraces descend from the churchyard to rectilinear fishponds linked by a canalized, stone-lined stream, in the valley bottom. From the north-east corner of the house a raised walk leads down into the gardens, over a bridge (now collapsed, but formerly over a walk leading to the terraces), past the fishponds, and up ruined steps to a raised look-out platform or gazebo. John Aubrey, the famous seventeenth-century antiquary, much enjoyed his sojourns with his relations at Llantrithyd, and even today it is possible to see why.

## Fragments

Some houses of the period retain fragments of contemporary gardens such as walling, a garden building, or just earthworks in farmland. One of the most interesting remnants of this kind is

*The raised walk in the ruined gardens of Llantrithyd Place, S. Glamorgan. These once superb gardens are thought to date from the Elizabethan period (Photograph: author).*

Old Gwernyfed (Powys), built at the beginning of the seventeenth century by Sir David Williams. The remains of a sophisticated and complex garden lie in pasture to the north-east of the house, with earthworks of a raised terrace walk, a formal quartered garden with a central feature, terracing, and rectilinear ponds (now dry), one with small artificial islands. On the far side of the quartered garden is a stone gateway with fine ball-topped gateposts in the ruined garden wall. Flanking the front of the house are two delightful circular dovecots which combined practical use with decoration.

The large Tudor terraces built out over the steep drop next to Plas Machen (Gwent), home of a branch of the Morgans of Tredegar, survive. The house was built in about 1490 and enlarged in the early sixteenth century. Integrated into the scheme is a long fishpond parallel to the terraces in the valley below. There are remains of walled gardens of this period at Vaynol Old Hall (Gwynedd), and these incorporate a gateway inscribed 1634 T W K (Thomas and Katherine Williams) with 'YE MYSTIC GARDEN FOLD ME CLOSE I LOVE THEE WELL' written around the inner arch. At Cefn Tilla (Gwent) some terracing and walling remain of a seventeenth-century garden, and a contemporary gateway in the south wall is called Fairfax's Arch, named after the Parliamentary general who besieged Raglan Castle in 1646, and who had his headquarters at Cefn Tilla. Excavations and survey in the walled enclosures to the south of the Tudor semi-fortified mansion of Llancaiach Fawr (M. Glamorgan), home of the Prichard family, have revealed garden layouts of paths and flowerbeds, and there are plans to recreate them.

A tantalizing gap in our knowledge of the period is that of the gardens of Sir Richard Clough of Denbighshire, a rich merchant who was influenced by the houses he had seen in the Low Countries. He built the first brick houses in Wales, Plas Clough and Bachegraig (both in Clwyd), in the 1560s, but whether their gardens were in a matching continental style is unclear. A nineteenth-century drawing of an 'old painting' of Maenan Abbey, another of his houses, shows a small fenced garden with formal beds and standard trees or shrubs, and Richard Fenton's description of Bachegraig in the early nineteenth century says that 'The most uniform and handsomest front is towards a Garden, or perhaps what was once a bowling green, to the East'. Farm buildings now obscure most of this area.

One of the most advanced houses of the early seventeenth century in Wales was Plas Teg (Clwyd), built in about 1610 for Sir John Trevor, a successful courtier. An undated, probably eighteenth-century drawing shows that the sophisticated symmetrical plan of the house was matched outside by a forecourt with an ornamental gateway and two corner pavilions, further walled enclosures and an

The refined symmetry of handsome Plas Teg, Clwyd, built in 1610, was originally matched by formal gardens (Photograph: author).

The turf-covered remains of the early seventeenth-century formal gardens at Old Gwernyfed, Powys. All that survives upstanding is a single gateway (Photograph: author).

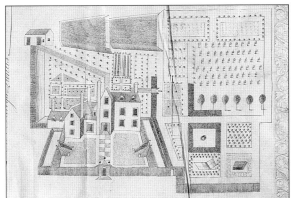

A detail from a map of Plas Llanbedr estate, Clwyd, of 1744, showing formal walled gardens (By courtesy of the National Library of Wales).

avenue on the main axis of the house. Of all this only one small ruined pavilion survives, and there is evidence that the garden very soon fell into decay after it was made. On the hillside above the back of the house – now in farmland – stand the ruined stone walls of a large walled garden.

Of statuary and fountains from the period very little survives. Sundials were popular, and some are known from Welsh gardens. At Coldbrook (Gwent) there was one in the grounds inscribed '1630 Long liffe to king Charles', and in front of Golden Grove (Clwyd) is one with a date of 1590 . At Llanfihangel Court (Gwent) there is a sundial set into a wall of the house inscribed 'N.A. [Nicholas Arnold] 1627'.

# Nectarines, Figs and Apricots

Some important gardens of the Tudor and early Stuart periods in Wales are only known through records, which indicate a high degree of horticultural knowledge at some great houses. At Llewenny Hall (Clwyd), now nearly all

demolished, Sir John Salusbury (1567-1612) recorded the plants in his garden, with their provenance, in 1596, 1607, and again in 1608. Gwydir (Gwynedd) was the home of the Wynns, the most important family in north Wales during this period. In the late sixteenth to early seventeenth century, the time of Sir John Wynn, it is known that there was a 'labyrinth', or maze, in the garden. Sir John's son wrote to him from France in 1613 suggesting that oranges and lemons would grow well at Gwydir. In 1618 Sir John's brother-in-law wrote from London that he would send nectarine and fig trees, and in 1625 he was sent bay plants and 'slivings' of tamarisk from Penrhyn (Gwynedd). Nothing is left of these important gardens, which have been overlain by many subsequent ones. Thomas Pennant, in his Tours in Wales (1778), mentioned that there had been a summerhouse on the hill above the house, built by Sir John, 'who had a classical taste', in 1604, and 'lately' demolished. An inscription in Welsh over the door indicated that this was intended to dominate the surrounding land, and was to be 'a second paradise, a fair bank, a palace of royalty'.

At the other end of Wales, at Troy House, the large walled garden is older than the Restoration mansion. Over the doorway to the entrance lobby is a heraldic panel with the initials E C S – Elizabeth and Charles Somerset – and the date 1611. Of this once highly productive garden, only the high stone walls, in which are set two bee boles, and covered entrance remain. When King Charles I was staying at Raglan Castle in 1645 with the marquis of Worcester, the marquis's brother, Sir Thomas Somerset, sent the king a present from Troy of some apricots grown in his gardens. For, as the marquis said,

*The gateway into the early seventeenth-century walled garden at Troy House, Gwent (Photograph by Wilma Allan).*

'Sir Thomas being a compleat Gentleman of himself, delighted himself much in fine gardens and orchards'. The king was astonished at and delighted with this present.

## 'Upon this Primrose Hill': Castle Gardens

By the sixteenth century most castles in Wales had fallen into ruin, abandoned by their owners in favour of more comfortable accommodation. Those that remained inhabited were modernized to become stately castle-like mansions rather than true fortresses. Some of the most powerful families in Wales followed this course, including the Somerset family at Raglan, the Stradlings at St Donat's, the Herberts at Cardiff, and the Perrots at Carew (Dyfed) and Laugharne (Dyfed). By the end of the sixteenth century Chirk Castle was in the hands of the Myddleton family, who have lived there ever since. From both remains and records we know that handsome gardens were made at these castles, and that those at Chirk and St Donat's were on a grand scale, incorporating many Renaissance features. But by far the most ambitious and magnificent, and the best preserved castle gardens of this period are those of Raglan Castle (see p. 22).

As for Chirk, the castle has had a remarkable series of gardens covering most styles from the early seventeenth century to the present day. They are

*Carew Castle, Dyfed, which was given formal gardens by Sir John Perrot in the late sixteenth century. (By courtesy of Dyfed County Council).*

Right: *Whitehurst Gardens, Chirk, formerly the great walled garden of Chirk Castle (Photograph: author).* Above: *The gardens were built by Sir Thomas Myddelton, 1586-1666 (National Trust Photographic Library).*

exceptionally well documented, and on the ground fragments remain from each period that graphically indicate the grandeur and sophistication of the layouts. In 1613 three shillings were paid for gooseberry, strawberry and blackberry plants, two shillings were paid to three men for mowing the bowling alley, and five shillings were paid for five dozen quinces. Where this early garden and bowling alley were is not known, but the next stage in development can still be seen at Whitehurst Gardens, two miles (3.2km) to the north of Chirk village. In about 1651 Sir Thomas Myddelton (1586-1666) built a walled garden here, which still survives. It has an unusual layout, with four curving walls one above the other on a south-facing slope, and a circular mount in the south-west corner. The appearance of this garden in the early eighteenth century is clearly shown in the top left-hand corner of Thomas Badeslade's magnificent 1735 engraving of 'The West Prospect of Chirk Castle', with its walls, formal layout, and wooded mount topped by a single tree.

During the 1650s the Chirk garden was stocked with liquorice plants, vines, damsons, red currants, gooseberries, a fig tree (brought from Lancashire), apples, pears, angelica, and other unspecified plants. There were several summer houses, part of one of which survives, and in 1653 a blacksmith was

paid for '10 weathercocks for the newe sum[mer] houses at the garden'. The garden seems to have been used as a handy place of refreshment by passing judges; there are several records of paying for beer and biscuits for them at the garden. It can have been little different from its description in 1684 by Thomas Dineley, in *The Beaufort Progress*: 'an admirable walled garden of trees plants and flowers and herbs of the greatest variety as well forreigne as of Great Britain, orrenge and lemon trees the sensitive plant and where in a Banquetting house a collation of choice fruit and wines was lodged by the sayd Sr Richard Middleton to entertein his Grace'.

Sir Thomas Myddelton also made a terraced garden beneath the east front of the castle, as recorded in a Latin inscription on a stone tablet in the garden: 'Horti/Voluptatis, amaenitatisque/Causa Parati/Thom. Myddelton/Milite/1653'. This garden, with two gazebos that may be late seventeenth century in date, is shown in a watercolour sketch of 1720 by Peter Tillemans.

That Sir Thomas Myddelton was a keen horticulturalist is also shown by his book buying. In 1652 he acquired 'Penkinson's Herball' [*Theatrum Botanicum* by John Parkinson (1640)], and in 1655 Parkinson's *Paradisi in sole Paradisus Terrestris* (1629).

*The restored terracing at St Donat's Castle, S. Glamorgan, which is of Tudor origin (Photograph: author).*

On the southern seaboard at St Donat's Castle, although much altered and modernized in the twentieth century, the site retains the structure of its Tudor terraced gardens, which lie on the steep slope between the castle and the sea. The terracing, with its massive retaining walls, doorways and steps, are all that remain of the gardens that were made by Sir Thomas Stradling and his son Sir Edward during the sixteenth century. Sir Edward was a cultured and well travelled man, and his time spent in Rome may have influenced his gardens, which are known to have included statues of Roman emperors. There was also a celebrated rose garden, said in a poem by Thomas Leyshon to be lovely enough to draw Neptune and Thetis from their deep salt-water haunts. Also recorded were a herb garden, vineyard and deer park, with an earlier watch-tower or eyrie on the ridge to the west, which may well have been used as a banqueting house-cum-gazebo. The 'Tudor' garden, with its 'Queen's beasts' on stone columns, an idea taken from Henry VIII's garden at Hampton Court, is the work of Morgan Stuart Williams in the early twentieth century.

The gardens at Cardiff Castle were much smaller, fitted into courts within the enclosure of the castle. Henry Herbert, who held the castle from 1570 to 1601, made it into a luxurious residence by extensive rebuilding. Of his gardens nothing remains, but Rice Merrick's description of the castle in about 1580 indicates where they were. The previous 'chiefest garden', at the south end of the domestic apartments on the west side of the castle enclosure, was turned into a kitchen garden, and two new pleasure gardens were made to the north, one in front of the hall block and the other in the 'Inner Court', between the apartments and the ditch of the motte. This one was overlooked by the 'Ladies Walk', on top of the west curtain wall.

Carew and Laugharne Castles, both in picturesque seaside locations, lie in ruins now, and very little of their gardens survives above ground. But both were given layouts with Renaissance features. Sir John Perrot (d. 1592), after he had been granted Laugharne castle in 1584, turned it into a grand mansion, with decorative cobbling and a fountain in the courtyard, and a garden in the outer ward. At Carew Sir John added a large north wing between 1588 and 1592, with great oriel windows looking out over the tidal inlet. He also piped water to the kitchen and brewhouse from a fountain in the garden. A 1592 survey indicates a complex of gardens and courts, orchards and dovecot. The eastern approach leads through two grass courts flanked by features including gardens, a tiny deer park to the north and stables and a garden to the west. Some details of all this have been found by excavation, and enclosures can be made out as stumps of ruined walls and banks to the east of the castle.

Documentary records give fleeting glimpses of further castle gardens of the period, all long since disappeared. At Newcastle Emlyn (Dyfed), where only the ruined gatehouse and parts of the walls remain, Sir Rhys ap Thomas (d. 1525) rebuilt the castle as a mansion in the early sixteenth century, and George Owen recorded a 'peece of grownde' called the 'Castell Garden' outside the castle moat in 1594. The bird's-eye view of Conwy, painted in about 1600 (p. 21), shows the castle garden in the east barbican still in existence. Finally, the poet John Donne (1573-1631) showed his appreciation of the surroundings of Montgomery Castle (Powys) in a poem entitled 'The Primrose, being at Montgomery Castle, upon the hill, on which it is situate'

*Upon this Primrose hill,*
*Where, if Heav'n would distil*
*A shoure of raine, each severall drop might goe*
*To his owne primrose, and grow Manna so;*

# Town Gardens

The painting of Conwy of about 1600 shows small gardens, albeit depicted schematically, behind most of the houses in the walled town, with orchards filling most of the spaces

*A painting of Conwy in about 1600, showing the castle and walled town. Gardens can be seen attached to each house, and near the top are the large house and garden of Plas Mawr (By courtesy of the marquis of Salisbury).*

between the houses and the town wall. The garden of the large house near the west end of the town stands out as being much larger than the rest. This is Plas Mawr, built between 1576 and 1580 by Robert Wynn, a son of John ap Meredith of Gwydir. Although the gardens have gone, the house and its inner courtyard remain remarkably intact. The comparative sophistication of this house is shown by the raised terrace, part of which is contemporary with the house. There was originally a small gazebo, which was removed when the south-west section of the terrace was added in the late eighteenth or early nineteenth century.

There is further evidence for the existence of town gardens in the sixteenth and early seventeenth centuries, in the form of maps by John Speed, published in 1610. The map of Flint (Clwyd), a planned garrison town established by Edward I in the late thirteenth century, is typical. It shows rudimentary gardens behind the houses, tree-lined roads, and a large central tree. Similar enclosures are shown on Speed's maps of other towns, such as

Carmarthen (Dyfed), Brecon (Powys) and Cardiff, while a later map (1686) of Chepstow (Gwent) shows town gardens and orchards in some detail. Although these maps give very little information on the exact layout of the gardens, they do show that they were geometrical, with trees in straight rows, square or rectangular beds, and enclosing walls, fences or hedges.

*Rudimentary gardens are depicted behind the houses in this 1610 plan of Flint town and castle by John Speed (By courtesy of the National Library of Wales).*

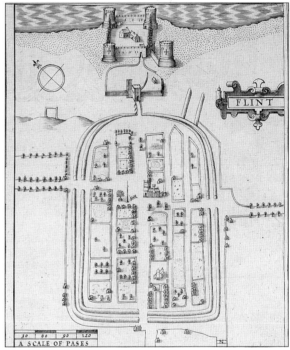

*The town gardens and orchards are clearly illustrated on this 1686 map of Chepstow by Jacob Millerd (By permission of Newport Borough Libraries).*

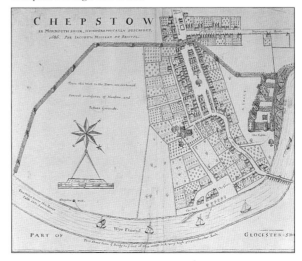

# Raglan Castle

Beneath the greensward which surrounds Raglan Castle lie the greatest gardens in Wales of the Tudor and early Stuart periods. Very few gardens of high calibre survive in Britain from this period, making the unaltered Raglan gardens all the more important. Although only the structure of the gardens is visible, historical sources make it possible to build up a much more detailed picture of their original appearance.

The gardens were made by the third and fourth earls of Worcester, between 1549 and 1628, and continued in use until the castle was abandoned after the Civil War siege by Parliamentarians in 1646. The earls of Worcester were among the most powerful and wealthy barons in the land, virtual 'rulers' of south Wales, and prominent at the courts of Elizabeth I, James I and Charles I.

When William Somerset (1527?-89) became the third earl of Worcester in 1549 he spent lavishly on Raglan Castle, converting it into a 'stately castle-like house' which was 'accounted, when in its splendour, one of the fairest buildings in England'. He made grand Renaissance gardens to complement his palace. Within the castle, in what is now called the Fountain Court, he installed a 'pleasant marble fountain. called the White Horse, continually running with a clear water'. A poem of 1587 mentions it and other features of the gardens:

*An aerial view of Raglan Castle from the west, showing the garden terraces built and maintained by the third and fourth earls of Worcester.*

*The curious knots, wrought all with edged toole,*
*The stately Tower, that looks ore Pond and Poole:*
*The fountain trim, that runs both day and night,*
*Doth yeeld in show a rare and noble sight.*

To the north-west of the castle, where the ground slopes steeply, the third earl built up three long terraces. These were backed by high walls and reached by steps at their western end. They can still be seen, turf-covered, surrounded by a massive retaining wall with a central projection. The finding of some primitive stone balustrading at the castle makes it likely that the tops of the terrace walls were balustraded, giving the gardens a very Italianate feel, rather like the terraces at Powis Castle, which are more than a hundred years later. The terraces would have been laid out with straight paths and rectilinear beds of 'curious knots', which were interwoven patterns of low-growing aromatic shrubs such as santolina and germander. To complete the picture on this side of the castle there was a large lake below the terraces, called the 'great poole' on a map by Laurence Smythe of 1652. This 'fish pond of many acres of land' was created by the massive earthen dam to the south-west of the terraces, through which the Wilcae Brook now runs. In function it was both utilitarian, 'where they had store of very great carps, and other large fish', and ornamental. From the terraces or the long gallery the view out over the lake to the deer park and in the distance the Black Mountains, would have been very beautiful.

To the south-west of the castle there was a square 'garden plot' with a raised walk around two sides, which can be seen at the top of the terraces. Below it, reached by steps which are still there, was a large garden terrace, clearly visible in the field below, overlooking a hopyard and orchard. Curving around the outside of the keep's moat is a raised bowling green, also thought to be the work of the third earl.

Thus in 1589 Edward, fourth earl of Worcester (1563-1628), inherited extensive and sophisticated gardens. During the next forty years he was to add further refinements and features that were fashionable in the highest court circles in which he moved. Summerhouses were built on the terraces, and the footings of one of them are visible at the western end of the top terrace. A curving walk was made between the keep's moat and the bowling green, with fifteen niches in its wall, in which stood statues of Roman emperors. The niches were decorated with patterns of shells set in coloured plaster. The emperors have long since gone, but the

niches are still there, and a careful examination will reveal remnants of the coloured plasterwork and shellwork patterns.

The Laurence Smythe map clearly shows a most exciting and unusual feature at the head of the 'great poole': a rectangular area divided into diamond-shaped and triangular islands by narrow water channels, with a central built feature. This 'water parterre' of 'divers artificial islands and walks' was added by the fourth earl, probably in the early years of the seventeenth century, when water parterres were fashionable in high court circles. Very few remain, which makes the survival of Raglan's, as boggy ditches and raised banks in pasture, all the more remarkable. To the south of the castle, in the valley bottom below the dam, was another simpler water garden of four square islands, which may have been the precursor of the more complex one. This also survives in pasture.

*William Somerset, third earl of Worcester, who was largely responsible for the creation of the gardens at Raglan.*

*Laurence Smythe's plan of Raglan, 1652, showing the terraces, 'great poole', and two formal water gardens (By kind permission of the duke of Beaufort).*

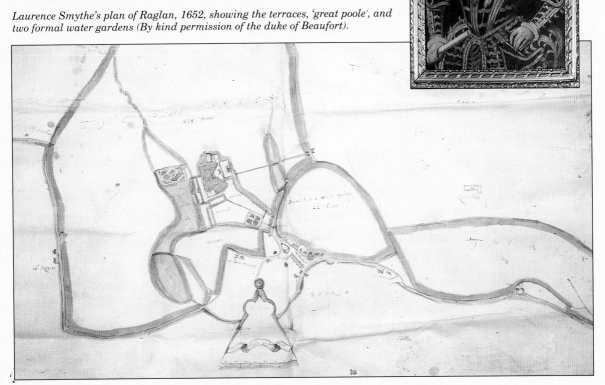

# Plantations and Parks

Beyond the immediate surroundings of castle and home, there is evidence that the landed gentry of the Tudor and early Stuart age did not neglect the adornment of their land. Although planting of deciduous and coniferous trees was primarily for commercial purposes it did include an ornamental element. In 1603 George Owen stated that 'prettie groves of woode, as oake, ashe, mapple, Elme, and such like, and diverse rare tymber, as the pyne aple tree [presumably Scots pine], the spruse, and fyrre trees, the Mulbery tree and others' were planted around 'houses of accompte'. Towards the end of the century new introductions began to trickle in from North America, and 'the Firre tree', probably *Pinus strobus*, is recorded by Roch Church (1612) in Pembrokeshire:

*'Master Thomas Bowen of Trefloyne in the County of Pembroke. had about fifteene or sixteene years past [about 1596] manie young and small plants of this kind brought him home by saylers from the Newfound land, with some of the earth wherein they did formerly grow, and planted them together with the said earth in convenient places about his house, where they have since so well prospered that many of them at this present are about foure foot in circuit, and also very high and tapering'.*

However, exotic conifers remained rare in Wales until the mid seventeenth century, by which time Sir Thomas Hanmer of Bettisfield noted in his *Garden Book*, that Scots pine, Norway spruce, European larch, cypress and cedar were grown for ornamental planting in avenues, walks and groves.

Some deer parks were kept up, although many medieval ones were disparked during this period. A few new ones were made, such as that at Llanddowror (Dyfed), created by the Perrott family. The Somersets of Raglan Castle had two parks, one near the castle and a red deer park a few miles to the north, where a park lodge was built on the medieval moated site of Hen Gwrt. The Carnes at Ewenny Priory (M. Glamorgan) and the Stradlings at St Donat's Castle also had two deer parks each, one for fallow and one for red deer. From 17 known deer parks in Glamorgan in the sixteenth century, some of medieval origin, some Tudor, only those at Rhiwperra and Margam Abbey survived into the seventeenth century. The medieval deer park at Chirk Castle continued in use, and was enlarged at its southern end in 1675 to hold 500 deer. In his letter to a Mr Prichard at the castle, Sir Thomas Myddelton gave details of the proposed extension, including his hope that 'if I can get those little fields belonging to the Quakers I would have the pale come all the way to Chirk and to meet with the great gates'. The other Chirk deer park of Black Park, to the north, was also improved.

Top: *Hen Gwrt, Gwent, a medieval moated site on which there was a deer park lodge during the sixteenth and seventeenth centuries.*
Below: *This detail of John Speed's map of 1610, shows enclosed deer parks in mid Gwent, including that centred on Hen Gwrt (By courtesy of the National Library of Wales).*

# Chapter 3
# *Baroque Grandeur: 1660 to 1730*

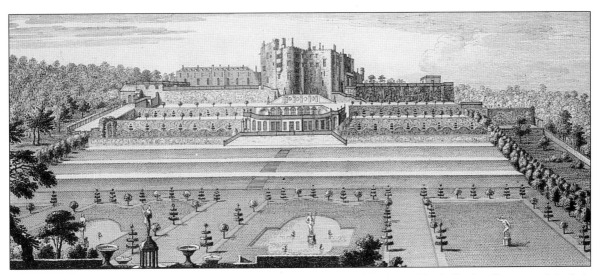

*An engraving of 1742 by Samuel and Nathaniel Buck, showing the formal gardens at Powis Castle still very much in their infancy (By courtesy of the National Library of Wales).*

The seventy or so years following the Restoration of King Charles II in 1660 saw the re-emergence of the great families of Wales from the upheavals of the Civil Wars (1642-48), battered but not bowed. Fines were paid, damage repaired, and the most powerful families set about amassing more land and wealth. At the beginning of the period it was said that it was easier to find 50 Welsh gentlemen with an income of £50 a year than five with £100. In 1668 Sir Thomas Hanmer, one of the most noted horticulturalists of his day, wrote to John Evelyn about gardens in Wales, saying 'I know not of any noble ones; wee have within these few yeares in Flintshire and some other shires near to mee many gentlemen that have upon my instigation & persuation fallen to plant both flowers & trees, and have pretty handsome little grounds, but no-body hath adventured upon large spatious ones, with costly fountains or other waterworkes, or groves or great parterres, etc.'.

By the early eighteenth century this situation had changed quite significantly, and some landowners, through land acquisition, judicious marriage to heiresses, improvements on their estates, and in some cases mineral exploitation and industrial enterprise, had vastly increased their wealth. Sir Watkin Williams Wynn of Wynnstay (Clwyd) led the field with an annual income of

nearly £20,000 by 1736, the Morgans of Tredegar followed with £10,000 a year, and many of the great families, including the Myddeltons of Chirk Castle, Mostyns of Mostyn Hall, Herberts of Powis Castle (Powys), Vaughans of Golden Grove (Dyfed), Mansels of Margam Abbey (W. Glamorgan), and Lewises of The Van had between £1,000 and £5,000 a year.

The trend towards amalgamation, and the squeezing out of smaller owners, was concentrated in the lowland parts of Wales, as one early eighteenth-century rhyme shows:

*Alas alas poor Radnorshire*
*Never a park, not even a deer,*
*Never a squire of five hundred a year*
*Save Richard Fowler of Abbey Cwm-hir.*

Most of Wales remained difficult of access. Even the redoubtable Celia Fiennes only ventured as far as Hawarden and Holywell (Clwyd) in 1698. Those who penetrated further were not appreciative of the scenery. Ned Ward described Wales as 'the fag-end of creation; the very rubbish of Noah's flood'. Daniel Defoe in 1726 saw only 'horrid rocks and precipices' in upland south Wales, but did venture along the southern coastal plain as far as Pembrokeshire. It was in the lowland areas of the Marches, and of north-east and south-east Wales that most gardens of the period were made. Some were very grand, and remarkably a few survive.

This was the era of the spacious baroque garden, introduced to royalty and the upper echelons of society from the Continent. Gardens were still formal and enclosed, but their scale increased enormously, with terracing, wide gravel walks, parterres, groves, avenues, canals, fountains and statues. Walks and avenues continued the axes of houses into the gardens and out across the landscape beyond, bold statements of ownership and domination. Very few in Wales could afford this kind of magnificence, and there is, for example, no evidence that George London and Henry Wise – who laid out so many grand English gardens – worked in the Principality. Nevertheless, a few grand baroque gardens were certainly created, most notably at Chirk, Powis (see p. 26), Erddig (see p. 34), and Tredegar House. Had Sir Thomas Hanmer lived longer he might have enthused to John Evelyn about these 'large spatious' gardens lately established in Wales.

Some fashionable ideas filtered through to the less wealthy and ambitious, and all over Wales baroque elements such as avenues, terraces, canals, and a modicum of axial planning were grafted on to existing ad hoc layouts. Avenues, generally of hardwoods such as oak, lime, or sweet chestnut, appear to have been popular, but many are known only from records. There are, for instance, paintings that show the avenue which ran from Troy House to Monmouth, and the great avenue from Margam

*A 1773 map of Picton Castle demesne, Dyfed, showing the avenue terminated by a summerhouse (By courtesy of the National Library of Wales).*

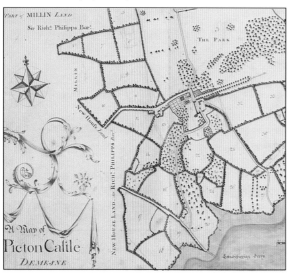

House to the sea, or old maps that show the avenues at Lawrenny (Dyfed) and Picton Castle (Dyfed).

Elsewhere there are some remarkable survivals which can be seen today, including the magnificent lime avenues at Mostyn Hall and Soughton Hall (Clwyd), and the sweet chestnut avenue at Llanfihangel Court (Gwent). Some have been preserved through continual replacement, such as the great oak avenue at Tredegar, and the pine avenues of Trewyn (Gwent) and Llangibby House (Gwent). A few other examples survived into the twentieth century, including the great walnut avenue at Gwernyfed (Powys), and the pine avenue at Llanfihangel Court. Fragments of others survive, such as an avenue of horse chestnuts at Itton Court (Gwent).

Of the few Welsh canals made in this period the chief survivor is that at Erddig. That at Nerquis Hall (Clwyd), dating to around 1700, is silted up, and that at Pontypool Park (Gwent), was removed in nineteenth-century landscaping.

# Sir Thomas Hanmer

**S**ir Thomas Hanmer (1612-78) of Bettisfield (Clwyd) was Wales's greatest horticulturalist, and one of the finest of his day in Britain. He moved in elevated horticultural circles; King Charles II's gardener John Rose, for example, sent two vines (a Lombardy vine and 'the right Rhenish grape') to Bettisfield, and John Evelyn was a friend. From his *Garden Book* (1659), together with his own notes on the garden at Bettisfield, and the writing of some of his friends, in particular his good friend John Rea, Hanmer emerges as a man of the widest knowledge, who had what John Rea called an 'incomparable collection' of plants in his garden.

*Sir Anthony Van Dyck's portrait of Sir Thomas Hanmer of Bettisfield, Clwyd: Wales's greatest horticulturalist (By kind permission of the Trustees of the Weston Park Foundation: photograph by Courtauld Institute of Art).*

This garden was simpler than the grandiose kind described in his *Garden Book*, with a 'great' vineyard. Although all has completely disappeared, a rough picture of its layout and contents can be worked out from Hanmer's notes. Against the wall were many fruit trees and an outer border. The interior was filled with small rectilinear beds edged with boards, between which were gravel and turf paths. Sir Thomas listed the plants in the four central beds, which were planted in rows. Tulips, his favourite flowers, dominated the first bed, with colchicums and anemones in the corners; in the second were crown imperials, irises and daffodils; the third was mainly planted with varieties of *Narcissus*, but included other plants such as grey and black fritillaries; and the fourth was full of tulips. Sir Thomas's expertise with tulips was well known in his day, and among the many varieties he grew were the famous 'Viceroy' and 'Agate Hanmer' which he probably raised himself. His eye for a good plant led him to prophesy a great future for the cedar of Lebanon, which is first mentioned in this country in his *Garden Book*.

# Llannerch: 'Foreign Outrageously Unnatural Style'

Had the gardens at Llannerch (Clwyd) survived, they would undoubtedly rival for drama those of Powis Castle. Fortunately, we know something of their appearance from a huge anonymous painting of the gardens, thought to date from 1662, of which there are two slightly different versions. The paintings show a series of walled enclosures stepping down the steep hillside above the River Clwyd, ending with a circular pool in the valley bottom, with a fountain of Neptune in the centre. Within the gardens are cypresses, wall fruit, formal plantations, further pools and fountains, a grotto and cascade, steps and gazebos. Such is the grandeur of the scheme, that if there were not corroborating evidence for its existence, it would be tempting to suggest that it was pure fantasy and had never existed.

*This painting of about 1662 gives a bird's eye view of the once spectacular gardens built on terraces below the house at Llannerch. The gardens, complete with walled enclosures and exotic water tricks, were destroyed in the Victorian period, and now lie buried beneath the turf (By kind permission of Yale Center for British Art, Paul Mellon Collection).*

To understand why such an exotic garden, with Italianate water tricks and hydraulic statues, was made in north Wales it is necessary to know something of its maker, Mutton Davies. He was the son of Robert Davies (d. 1666) of nearby Gwysaney, and Anne Mutton of Llannerch, daughter of a prosperous judge, Sir Peter Mutton, who built the house at the beginning of the seventeenth century. In 1654, Davies went abroad on the Grand Tour, and visited Italy. Gardens such as Pratolino near Florence must have impressed him, and when he returned home in 1658 and took over Llannerch he was sufficiently wealthy to create an Italianate terraced garden there. As for the water tricks, some are recorded: Philip Yorke (1743-1804) of Erddig knew a sundial there which spouted water in one's face, and on which was written

*Alas! my friend, time soon will overtake you; And if you do not cry, by G – d I'll make you.*

A contemporary Welsh poem by Ffoulk Wynn praises the house and then goes on to descibe the gardens. Translated, it reads

*Elegantly he diverted streams of cold water into his gardens and, praise be, he can wander in a great garden which he made, in the grounds about his mansion, and costly are his devices* [or tricks].

The Llannerch gardens were still there at the beginning of the nineteenth century, and were described in 1812 as having 'formal walks, clipt trees, and hydraulic statues'. They were destroyed later in the Victorian period, and hence one of the most spectacular and outlandish gardens in Wales has sunk beneath the turf.

# 'Large Spatious Ones': Grand Baroque Gardens

**M**any of the grand formal gardens and parks created in this period survived right through the eighteenth century, and some even to the present day. Ironically, their survival is due either to the neglect or the conservatism of their owners. The outstanding example of survival through conservatism is Erddig (p. 34), and the outstanding example of survival through neglect is Powis Castle (p. 30).

## Chirk Castle

Many of the trees in the park at Chirk had been cut down in 1659 when the castle was taken by Parliament. But, as Thomas Dineley's description of 1684 and various castle accounts show, the gardens continued to be well kept up after the Civil War, and large-scale tree planting was carried out in the park from the early 1660s onwards, including Scots pine, sycamore, elm and oak. Gazebos and a sundial (1696) were added to the garden east of the castle, and honeysuckles are recorded in the courtyard in the 1690s.

The great change to a grand baroque layout came in the early 1700s. In June 1708 payments were being made for 'Turff for ye sloops & verges in ye Parteare of ye Castle fflower de Luce' (a parterre in the shape of a fleur de lis), and for 'Raiseing Gravell for ye walkes about ye fflower de Luce in ye new garden'. Thomas Badeslade's two views of the castle of 1735 give a general idea of the new layout. The formal gardens had spacious terraced lawns and gravel paths flanked by widely spaced trees within walled or hedged compartments. The main axes extended out into the park as avenues or rides. At a distance from the castle was a small building, the 'Cold Bath'.

*The 'North-East Prospect of Chirk Castle', 1735, by Thomas Badeslade, showing the great baroque gatescreen in its original position (By courtesy of the National Library of Wales).*

The most important axis was on the north side, leading from a formal lake up to the main entrance. It was Robert Myddelton (1678-1733) who in 1712 commissioned Robert Davies, the outstanding ironsmith from Bersham, to make the great baroque wrought-iron gatescreen to close the forecourt on this side. It was set up between 1718 and 1720, but was moved in later landscaping, and now stands at the entrance to the park. The forecourt was adorned with two large lead classical statues of Hercules and Mars. On 14 January 1720, £7 16s. was paid to convey them from London to the castle. When formal gardens went out of fashion they were

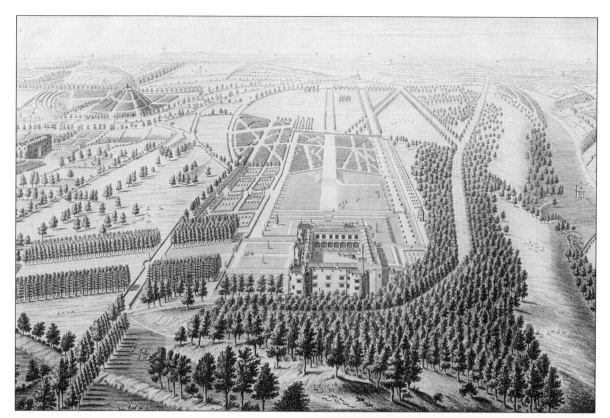

Above: *An engraving by Thomas Badeslade of the 'West Prospect of Chirk Castle', 1735, showing the new formal layout of the gardens (By courtesy of the National Library of Wales).*

Right: *The magnificent wrought-iron gates at Chirk, which originally stood in the forecourt north of the castle (By courtesy of the Wales Tourist Board).*

ditched in the park, but Hercules has been reinstated in the centre of the main east-west axis of the gardens. Wolves feature in the family coat of arms, and lead ones topped the gate piers; from 1680 to the 1730s a live one was kept in the dry ditch by the entrance. Robert Myddelton's was said to be 'pretty tame'.

The lifespan of this magnificent layout was short indeed – only some 45 years – and very little of it survives, apart from individual elements such as the gates, Hercules, and a sundial, none of which is in its original position. The main east-west axis remains as a cutting through Pleasure Ground Wood. On the north side all is swept away, and the formal lake has been landscaped so as to appear 'natural'. Most seventeenth- and early eighteenth-century trees have gone from the park, but a few hornbeams may be some of those planted in 1727, and two venerable larches in the shrubbery may also date from this period.

# Powis Castle

*The Italianate gardens at Powis Castle represent the most important and grandiose historic gardens in Wales (National Trust Photographic Library / Ian Shaw).*

Powis Castle has the most important and magnificent historic garden in Wales, and one of the best in Britain. For here survives a dramatic series of garden terraces built in the last years of the seventeenth century. Very few Italianate gardens of this kind were built in Britain, and even fewer remain. Of those that do Powis Castle's are the most complete and unaltered.

The castle stands on a gritstone ridge to the south of Welshpool, a few miles from the Welsh border. In origin it is medieval, but in 1587 it was bought by Sir Edward Herbert, and since then has been a stately residence of the Herbert family rather than a military stronghold. Already in 1684, when Thomas Dineley sketched the castle for his *Beaufort Progress*, some Renaissance features had been added around the castle. On the north-east side were flights of steps up to the entrance, with a balustraded terrace and summerhouse above them. On the other side of the castle Dineley's sketch of the forecourt shows a central fountain and a balustraded raised walk.

The great terraces on the steep slope below the castle were built by the first and second marquises of Powis in the last decade of the seventeenth

century, although they may have been begun earlier. Their architect was probably the Dutch-born William Winde (d. 1722) who was at the castle in 1697. Wealth from lead mines on the estate provided the means to undertake this massive scheme. The history of the castle at this time is complicated. The family was Catholic, and the first marquis (d. 1696) went into exile with James II to St Germain-en-laye, near Paris, which had magnificent Italianate terraced gardens. In 1695 Willem Hendrik van Nassau (1645-1709), of Zuylestein in Holland, was created earl of Rochford by his cousin, King William I, who also granted him the Powis estates. The earl, who has sometimes been credited with having made the terraces, spent most of his time in Holland and barely visited Powis Castle. It would appear, therefore, that the second marquis continued the work of his father after 1696 and completed the gardens 'in the wretched taste of St Germains en Laye', as Thomas Pennant later wrote, while the earl of Rochford was the supposed owner. The Herbert family regained their possessions in 1722.

Three long terraces, backed by brick walls and linked by flights of steps, were blasted out of the rock, and remain much as they were made. The central portions immediately below the castle are highly ornamented. Behind the upper terrace is a brick wall with five niches which once held marble busts. Along the top are huge clipped yews that are now so big they seem about to topple over the edge. These were planted soon after the terraces were made, and would originally have been kept small and neat, as they are shown on the 1742 engraving by the Buck brothers (p. 25). Likewise the huge yew hedge at the north end of the terraces started life small and geometrical.

The central part of the next terrace, called the Aviary Terrace, has eight brick arches (one blank) leading into a vaulted room once used as an aviary. The wall in front is topped by balustrading, lead urns, and four white-painted lead figures of a piper, shepherd, and shepherdesses, probably by the sculptor John Van Nost the elder. Beneath the centre of the Aviary Terrace is the main feature of

Top: *Statue of Pan on the third terrace, in front of the orangery at Powis (National Trust Photographic Library / Kevin J. Richardson).*
Bottom: *Huge clipped yews on the wall above the upper terrace at Powis, which appear small and neat on the Buck engraving of 1742, see p. 25 (Photograph: author).*

the third terrace, the orangery. This airy room, originally used to house orange trees in winter, is lit by six sash windows and a central door of 1665 that was moved here from the inner gate of the castle in about 1902. In front is a balustraded wall, below which is a steep slope known as the Apple Slope. This was originally turfed and scarped, as shown in the engraving by the Buck brothers, and was later an apple orchard. In the valley bottom, below the terraces, formal water gardens ornamented with clipped trees and statues were made sometime before 1742, but they were swept away in the next phase of alterations. The lead statue of Fame being carried by Pegasus, probably by the elder Van Nost and now in the forecourt, originally stood in these gardens. At the north end of the terraces stands a fine contemporary sculptural group, in lead and stone, of Hercules wrestling with the Hydra.

In the second half of the eighteenth century the family lived elsewhere, and the picture of the castle and gardens is one of neglect and decay. In 1784 John Byng commented that 'In the gardens, which were laid out in the wretched taste of steps, statues, and pavilions, not even the fruit is attended to; the ballustrades and terraces are falling down, and the horses graze on the parterres!!!'. It was at this time that the terraces had a narrow escape, for William Emes (see pp. 46-8) had a scheme for blowing them up with gunpowder and replacing them with a smooth turf slope. They were possibly reprieved by the intercession of Richard Payne Knight. In the early nineteenth century they were still 'grass-grown… descending in the forsaken grandeur of the last century'. Some landscaping was done by Emes, however, in the late 1770s. Apart from replacing the water gardens with a lawn, and preparing a new kitchen garden to the east of the castle he did some planting in the park and created the wooded area below the terraces known as the Wilderness.

*Hercules wrestling with the Hydra, on the north end of the terraces at Powis (By courtesy of the Wales Tourist Board).*

Between 1891 and 1952 the fourth earl of Powis and his wife embarked on a massive programme of clearance and planting of trees and shrubs, and the National Trust cares for and builds on this legacy.

## Tredegar House

In south Wales the most important house dating from the Restoration period is Tredegar House. It is a large brick mansion built around an earlier medieval and Tudor house between 1664 and 1672 by Sir William Morgan. The classical stable block and orangery were built slightly later (about 1690 to 1725) by John Morgan, and it was probably he who was largely responsible for the laying out of the park and gardens. Despite later landscaping and modern encroachments some of this baroque plan survives.

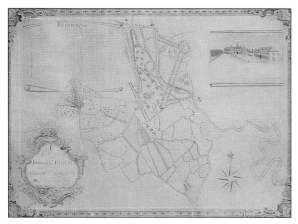

*A detail from a survey of Tredegar Park, Gwent, made by Robert Snell in about 1770, showing the formal layout of the avenues (By courtesy of the National Library of Wales).*

In the late seventeenth or early eighteenth century the three large garden enclosures to the west of the earlier house were modified, their walls rebuilt in brick, and the gardens were laid out, according to a nineteenth-century member of the family, the antiquary Octavius Morgan, 'in the Dutch style with many small beds, with winding walks and cut edgings between them'. The old labourer who gave him this information called the walks 'Turpentine' [serpentine]. Somewhere in the garden stood a sundial with the inscription 'latitude, 51 deg. 45 min., April 20th, 1698', which later stood at the head of the lake.

The 'Dutch' gardens were kept for almost a hundred years, until they were replanned in about 1790. The orangery was one of very few in Wales at this time (see also Powis Castle, p. 30). The orangery garden was covered with a thick layer of spoil from the making of the lake in about 1790, thus burying and preserving the older layout. This has recently been recovered by excavation to reveal a remarkably intricate formal layout of paths, beds,

a small mount, and a pair of inorganic parterres immediately in front of the orangery. The main central path was composed of coal dust bordered with crushed sea shells, and the patterns of the parterres were formed using different coloured materials such as crushed lime mortar, sea shells, brick and coal dust. The multi-coloured effect of this garden is now hard to imagine.

The main front of the house was given a magnificent baroque treatment similar to, and contemporary with, that at Chirk Castle, with wrought-iron gates and screens closing the inner of two courts. The gates were made by a Mr Edney of Bristol between 1713 and 1718, and cost the huge sum of £550. Beyond, the axis was continued by a great oak avenue stretching up the hill to the horizon. Much of this layout remains, with the forecourts and gates restored to their original appearance. Although truncated by the M4 motorway, 49 trees of the avenue – or 'The Walk' as it was known – remain, of which about four are thought to be original. An estate map of about 1770, by Robert Snell, shows how extensive the layout of avenues in the park was. An Iron Age hillfort to the north was used as an unusual focal point, with avenues radiating from it to the house and towards Bassaleg church. A further avenue of sweet chestnuts continued the main axis of the gardens southwards into the park.

## 'All Angles and Lines'

There were many gardens of a humbler variety, laid out by the gentry 'in the style of the time of King William, all angles and lines', as later a tourist described them. Among the most tantalizing disappearances are the gardens of Rhiwperra Castle. The house is a mock castle, similar to Plas Teg, built by Sir Thomas Morgan in 1626. It is now a ruined shell, which suffered the indignity of being burnt out twice, in 1783 and 1941. Thomas Dineley's sketch of 1684 shows a succession of forecourts in front of the house, and gardens were probably laid out either by Sir Charles Kemeys, in the late seventeenth or early eighteenth century, or by John Morgan, between 1706 and 1715. In about 1699 the gentleman architect William Winde, who also worked at Powis Castle and may have worked at Chirk Castle, wrote that he had successfully moved large trees in the orchard at Rhiwperra; perhaps his work extended to the whole garden. An estate map of 1764 shows forecourts, formal gardens, and a walk on the wooded hill behind, with a curious arrangement of parallel vistas, or 'lights' giving views of the gardens. The walk continues eastwards past a semi-circular alcove of yew, with a further 'light' below, to a circular mound on top of which was a square summerhouse. The mound was probably originally a medieval motte whose top was surrounded in the seventeenth century with a wall within which a two-storey summerhouse was built 'where the family used to drink tea in the summer time'.

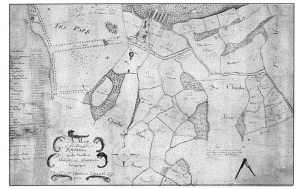

*A copy of a drawing of Rhiwperra Castle, M. Glamorgan, of about 1770, showing 'lights' and summerhouse on mound (By courtesy of the National Library of Wales).*

Tourists of the late eighteenth and early nineteenth centuries noted some 'outdated' garden survivals. Gloddaeth (Clwyd), for example, was described in 1792 as having been laid out by Colonel Sir Roger Mostyn (1624-90), with many trees, and 'according to the taste of his time, in straight walks, intersecting each other, or radiating from a center, distinguished by a statue. The upper walks, having fortunately a steep and stubborn rock for their basis, checked the modish propensity to rectitude'. In a letter to the countess of Fingall of 1768 'J.J.' writes that the gardens of Peniarth (Gwynedd) are 'in the style of the time of King William, all angles and lines. There is a long gravel walk shaded with a lofty and spacious arched avenue, another branching from it bordered by a full-grown filbert hedge'. At 'Old' Landshipping (Dyfed) there was a 'water folly by Mr Hancocke' in existence in 1693.

The Vaughan and later Stepney family houses of Machynys and Llanelli House (Dyfed) had an avenue about two miles (3.2km) long which 'began at the shrubbery of Llanelly House and led, almost unbroken… all the way to Machynis which was the eldest son's house in old days'. Edwinsford (Dyfed), now in ruins, appears to have had even more elaborate gardens. In 1803 a visitor reported that the house was 'beautified above, below, around, with leaden mercuries, shepherdesses, and sportsmen',

and that the gardens were 'in the genuine style of King William's reign, with all its absurdities, more interesting, as shewing us a specimen of that time, than if it were patched up with modern improvements; or a new villa, of the packing-case mode of building that now prevails. We rode through the long avenues of trees that extend from the house'. The statues survived at the house until the 1960s. Slebech (Dyfed) still has its long terraces overlooking the Eastern Cleddau estuary. Richard Fenton, writing in 1803 said that they were 'of Dutch origin, and much in vogue about a century ago', and that they were 'happily made subservient to fashionable luxury, by presenting walls of the best exposure for out-door fruit, and a series of noble walks and parterres'.

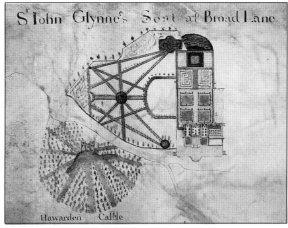

*A plan of Sir John Glynne's Seat at Broadlane Hall, Clwyd. showing the formal landscaping including Hawarden Castle, 1733 (By kind permission of the Clwyd County Record Office).*

Eighteenth-century estate maps, such as those for Mostyn Hall (1738), Broadlane Hall (1733), and Bodrhyddan (1756) in Clwyd, Pontypool Park (1752) and Trewyn (1726) in Gwent, and Picton Castle (1773) in Dyfed, show formal gardens and avenues. Most of these were subsequently swept away, but at Picton Castle a ride through the wood to the east of the house marks the late seventeenth- or early eighteenth-century avenue, and leads to the contemporary mount. In the west side of the mount is an enigmatic tunnel, possibly of the same date. On it stood a summerhouse, now gone, built in 1728 to a design by the London architect John James. Unfortunately, the 1773 map and a later painting give few indications of its appearance. At Trewyn the axis of the house is continued with terraces and steps leading down to an avenue which once stretched all the way to the River Monnow.

# Erddig

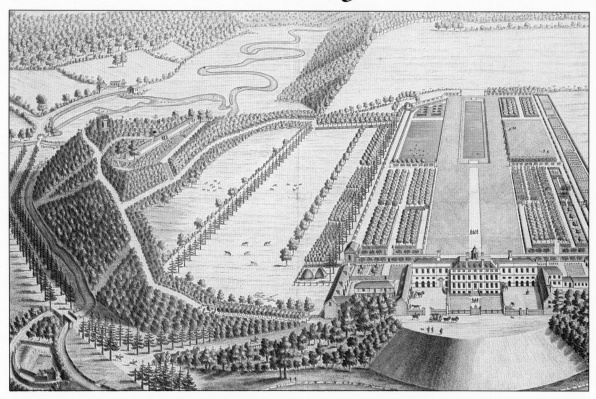

*An engraving by Thomas Badeslade of the west view of Erddig, 1740, showing the formal gardens created by John Meller between 1718 and 1733 (By courtesy of the National Library of Wales).*

Near the eastern border of Wales lies one of the most significant surviving gardens of the early eighteenth century in Britain, Erddig. Rescued from the brink of dereliction in the 1970s, it is now in the capable hands of the National Trust.

When Joshua Edisbury built his house just south of Wrexham between 1684 and 1687 there was little hint of the industrialization to come. The setting, on a high plateau above the valleys of the Black Brook and Clywedog river, was a rural one, with a Norman motte or castle mound to the north, and Saxon Wat's Dyke nearby. Before Edisbury's bankruptcy forced him to abandon Erddig at the beginning of the eighteenth century he had made a small formal walled garden to the east of the house. Today, its area is marked by a slight drop in level half-way to the canal, and rows of pleached limes.

The next owner, John Meller, who bought Erddig in 1716, was a London lawyer with more financial acumen than Edisbury. He lost no time in increasing the grandeur of Erddig. The house was extended to north and south, and Edisbury's garden

was swept away and replaced by a much more spacious formal walled garden almost Dutch in character. It is this garden whose bones have miraculously survived more or less intact to the present day. It was made between 1718 and 1733, when Meller died, by which time formal gardens were going out of fashion. Its layout soon after Meller's death is shown in Thomas Badeslade's engraving of 1740. The gardens were aligned on the main axis of the house, with a long central canal, a rectilinear pond to the north, a bowling green to the south, walls, summerhouses, scalloped yew hedges for beehives, and rows of trees (probably fruit trees). To the north was a long straight walk, possibly the 'Firr walk' referred to later, and the woods beyond were cut through with formal walks leading to a bowling green and the Norman motte, shown in the engraving with a tower on top, possibly a contemporary summerhouse. The entrance forecourt on the west side of the house was closed with handsome iron gates and screens made by the great Welsh smith Robert Davies, who had a forge at

Croes Foel nearby. In 1721 Meller's agent informed him that 'Robt. Davis the Smith has been ill of an Ague or the Iron Gate had been up before this time'. The gardens were soon planted, and a list of wall fruit in the kitchen garden in 1718 makes mouth-watering reading, including varieties such as 'Kanatian Peach', 'Blew Peralrigou Plumb', 'Scarlett Newington Nectorn', 'Gross Blanquett pare', 'Green Impardigall Do.' [plum], and 'Orange Apricock'. It is assumed that apples were grown free-standing. Many more fruit trees grew elsewhere in the garden, including in the 'Harty Choak Garden'.

The gardens continued to be improved by Meller's heir, his nephew Simon Yorke (d. 1767). In the 1750s letters tell of walks being gravelled, hedging, and other general gardening activities. But it was Simon's son Philip, who inherited in 1767, to whom we owe both the present appearance of the park and the preservation of the gardens. Philip I was a scholar and antiquary. He established the Yorke tradition of cherishing the family inheritance, and in particular Meller's gardens, which by Philip's day were decidedly old-fashioned. The landscape gardener, William Emes (pp. 46-8), who was brought in to improve the park to the north and west, was not allowed to touch them. The one concession to modernity around the house was to remove the stables and the Davies gates and screen from the west front to give an uninterrupted view of the park.

Between 1767 and 1789 Emes worked intermittently at Erddig. There was lavish planting to go with the newly excavated streams, and the formal walks in the woods to the north were softened. In 1778 Emes was paid for 'planting

scattered trees of tolerable size… at the foot of the Hill, west front'. His most unusual contribution was the building in 1774 of 'The Stone Cylinder in the Meadow', now called the 'Cup-and-Saucer'. The Black Brook flows over a cylindrical waterfall below which it runs through a tunnel, emerging under a fine rusticated arch. Philip's antiquarianism may have been the reason for the planting in the 1770s of a beech avenue which became known as the Cathedral Aisle, on a narrow ridge in the woods near the motte. Unfortunately, winter gales have accounted for all but a few of its members.

Generation after generation of head gardeners and other garden staff were recorded with portraits and poems by the Yorkes. For instance, James Phillips, appointed head gardener in 1841, was 'Old-fashioned, in his notions, he/With foreign names, did not agree'. The gardens reached something of a zenith in the Edwardian era, when the limes and rows of beeches flanking the canal (now gone) had achieved giant proportions, and planting was lavish. But there were only minor structural changes, such as the addition of stalagmitic fountains (1861) and the Edwardian parterre in front of the house, and the Irish yew walk and other Victorian planting on the south side of the garden. Walls connecting the two garden pavilions to the house were taken down in 1861 and curving gables added to the walls behind them. The wrought-iron gates and screen at the end of the canal, re-erected here in 1977, are attributed to Robert Davies. They were rescued from nearby Stansty Park in 1908, when they were repaired and erected at the Forest Lodge entrance to the park.

*The alcove summerhouse of Meller's garden, and the yew walk at Erddig (National Trust Photographic Library/Nick Carter).*

*The east front of Erddig, with the Victorian and later garden in the foreground (National Trust Photographic Library/Kevin J. Richardson).*

In terms of statuary and fountains, we have already seen a certain amount of evidence for Llannerch and Edwinsford. But by far the best survivals of statuary of the period are to be seen at Powis Castle (see p. 30), which has a magnificent collection, probably by the elder John Van Nost. In the forecourt is a huge lead group of Fame being carried by the winged horse Pegasus, while at the northern end of the terraces stands a magnificent composite group of Hercules (in lead) battling with the Hydra (in stone), based on a similar sculpture at Versailles by the seventeenth-century sculptor Pierre Puget. Lead rustic figures and a piper adorn the Aviary Terrace, and have recently been painted white, in accordance with the early eighteenth-century practice of painting lead statues in realistic colours or to imitate stone. In 1819 a visitor thought that the Fame group was actually stone.

Elsewhere, there were stone statues, including a musketeer, archer and pilgrim at Llantarnam Abbey (Gwent), and the formal gardens of Trefnannau Hall (Powys) were adorned with bronze statues of Hercules and Atlas 'who being naked, caused great offense to women and children passing down the road'. A 1743 picture of Kilgetty House shows statues and fountains in walled gardens with elaborate parterres. The gardens, the bones of which survive in farmland, were probably the work of the Philipps family in about 1725-26. The present ruined belvedere at the end of the central axis may have been part of this layout.

Thomas Dineley sketched many of the great houses of Wales in 1684 for the *Beaufort Progress* (an account of the duke of Beaufort's regal tour around Wales) – including Powis Castle, Chirk Castle, Mostyn Hall, Trawscoed (Dyfed), Rhiwperra, Troy House, Tredegar House, Picton Castle, and Margam Abbey – and the sketches provide valuable clues to the gardens of the period at these sites. Dineley's little vignettes show walled courtyards and gardens, sometimes with embellishments such as fountains, as at Powis Castle. At Margam a garden building and a formal pond are depicted. The building is presumably the banqueting house in which Sir Edward Mansel entertained the duke of Beaufort after the running down of two bucks.

The original pleasure gardens at Margam were probably made by Sir Thomas Mansel in the late sixteenth century, when he remodelled the Cistercian abbey to form a 'faire and sumptious house'. The appearance of the gardens and deer park in the late seventeenth century is recorded in two paintings which show a grand layout, very little of which survives. South of the house the paintings show four large rectangular fishponds, beyond which is a long broad avenue stretching almost to the sea. On the slope to the east are formal plantations, narrow ponds one above the other, and a bowling green backed by the classical banqueting house. To the west of the ponds are walled enclosures, two with formal gardens. The only remnants of this layout are the parallel ponds on the hill and the facade of the banqueting house, known as the 'four seasons' facade, which was removed when the building was demolished in the early nineteenth century and repositioned in a bizarre juxtaposition as the front of the gardener's cottage behind the orangery.

*A late seventeenth-century painting of Margam Old House, W. Glamorgan, showing the long garden avenue stretching towards the sea (Private collection: Photograph by the National Museum of Wales).*

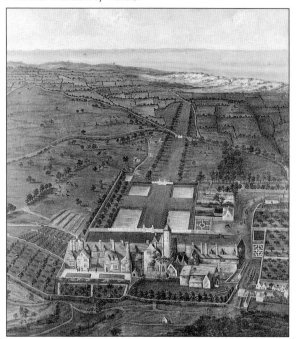

## 'Larg Chaney Oranges'

The most famous feature of the Margam gardens was the magnificent collection of citrus trees. It was known to have been in existence by 1711, when it was noted that the orange trees had been put out, which implies a greenhouse for winter storage. There are several versions of the origin of this collection, all fanciful. One has them as a gift from King Philip of Spain to Queen Elizabeth I, another from him to the king of Denmark, another from Sir Henry Wotton in Italy to Charles I. In all versions the trees end up at

Margam through shipwreck or capture, which part of the story may actually have been the case as Mansels were not noted for their scruples. In 1727 the greenhouse plants were catalogued by Joseph Kirkman, the gardener, who listed over fifty citrus trees, including 'Sittrons', 'Bergamots', lemons, limes, '10 Larg Chaney [China] Oranges, som 8 som 10 som 12 feet Diameter', '5 small Chaney Oranges about 4 feet Diameter', '13 Larg Sivel [Seville] Oranges about 7 som about 10 feet Diameter', some small Seville oranges, and some lemon stocks to be budded in pots. In 1753 the trees were recorded as having a spread of about 18 feet (5.4m) and a height of about 20 feet (6m). They were indeed among the most impressive in the country.

## 'The Old Style Itself': Survivors

Of gentry gardens of this period (1660-1730) that do survive, there are several outstanding examples. The first is Llanfihangel Court. John Arnold, Whig politician, rabid anti-Catholic, and arch-enemy of the duke of Beaufort, inherited the Tudor house from his horse-breeding father Nicholas in 1665, and set about giving it a grander, axially organized setting. A large oil painting of the park, thought to date from the 1680s, shows the formal layout he created. The gardens and park were carefully related to the house, whose front door was moved to the centre of the north side. Aligned on this door was a great north – south axis of terraces, steps, and two long avenues stretching out into the park, one of pines to the north, and one of sweet chestnuts to the south. Further avenues radiated out into the park. To the east of the house the painting shows a formal walled garden with pavilions in the corners. The terraces and steps north of the house remain, and the pine avenue survived into the 1940s. To the east, the walled garden was destroyed at the beginning of the nineteenth century, but one of the circular corner pavilions remains. To the south is the remarkable sweet chestnut avenue, over three hundred years old and still tottering on. To its north-west is a contemporary grove of sweet chestnuts, now mostly dead, said to have been planted to provide replacements for failures in the avenue.

The second important survivor is Llangedwyn Hall, in the Tanat valley (Clwyd). Here a magnificent series of brick terraces, similar to and roughly contemporary with those at Powis Castle, survive to the east of the house. They were made in the early eighteenth century at the same time as the Tudor house was remodelled by either Sir Edward Vaughan or Sir Watkin Williams of Wynnstay, who inherited the property in 1718. There is a contemporary painting which shows the layout more or less exactly as it is today. A lime avenue, which lasted until the 1970s, led from the road up to the forecourt in front of semi-circular steps up to the house. To the east of the house is the largest terrace, built out over the steep slope, with a gazebo at the far end. On the central axis of the terrace are two contemporary circular pools with simple jet fountains, supplied by iron pipes from a pond above the garden. Above are narrower terraces, while below, the ground is further divided by brick walls which originally flanked a long canal and bowling green. In 1907, when the garden was overrun with elaborate Victorian bedding it was said that 'No Capability Brown ever came to supplant its pleasant terraces with formless clumps and wearisome belts; no landscape gardener destroyed its honestly formal walks and replaced them with artificially-natural serpentines. This is not a garden after the old style, it is the old style itself'. It still is.

*One of the late seventeenth-century corner alcoves at Rhual, Clwyd, with original bench and wrought iron decoration (Photograph: author).*

Another delightful survivor of this period is Rhual (Clwyd), where a formal garden was added to a 1634 house in the late seventeenth century. The forecourt is flanked by corner brick alcoves, which retain their original curved benches and roofs topped with wrought-iron tulips. The brick garden walls are topped with contemporary wrought-iron ornaments. In the wooded area behind the house is that typically seventeenth-century feature, a bowling alley.

A survival of a slightly different kind is Llanmihangel Place (S. Glamorgan). This very fine gentry house is largely mid to late sixteenth century in date, but behind it, to the north, there remains a garden probably laid out by Humphrey Edwin, a London merchant, who had bought the property by 1681. It is a garden of eight acres (3.2ha), half formal terraced gardens divided into four quarters by paths lined with yews, and half former orchard. Around the edge are the remnants of a yew-lined perimeter path, and in the north-west corner is a traditional windbreak of massive pollarded sycamores. The avenue of huge yews down the main north-south axis is the main feature of the gardens, and in 1869 it was thought 'probably unrivalled in Wales'.

## 'To Look Abroad in to the Fields'

The summerhouses of Picton Castle, Kilgetty, and Rhiwperra Castle demonstrate that a desire to look out at the landscape beyond the park and garden developed in the baroque period. An interesting example of this was the addition of an upper storey to the thirteenth-century keep of Dinefwr Castle in the 1660s to make a summerhouse. This is probably the earliest instance in Wales of the reuse of a medieval castle for ornamental purposes.

*Newton House, Dinefwr, Dyfed, painted in about 1670, showing the formal gardens and summerhouse built on the ruined medieval castle (By kind permission of Lord Dynevor; photograph by the National Museum of Wales).*

To the few summerhouses can be added the artificial mount or viewing platform, used in sixteenth- and seventeenth-century gardens to 'look abroad in to the fields', as Francis Bacon (1561-1626) said. Mounts are not often encountered in Wales, possibly because the terrain usually made them unnecessary. The best surviving example is

probably that in the walled garden (at Whitehurst Gardens) of Chirk Castle, which is now very overgrown, but which, at the time of Badeslade's engraving (1735, p. 29), was formally laid out with paths cut through trees, and a fenced tree (? larch) on the top. Thomas Dineley gives a graphic account in the *Beaufort Progress* (1684) of Colonel Sir Roger Mostyn's mount at Mostyn Hall: on the afternoon of 24 July the duke of Beaufort and others were led into the gardens 'at ye corner of which upon a mount was placed a brass piece of Ordinance directed towards ye sea carrying these arms following [sketch] founded thereon'. All fired off the canon 'even to the last cartaridge of the noble Baronet's ammunition. Belonging to Mostyn House are a fair garden good Walks and excellent wall'd Fruit, not a little rare, so neer ye Salt Water'. A 1733 plan of 'Sir John Glynne's Seat at Broad Lane', in Hawarden (Clwyd) shows an axial layout with a mount, mazes, avenues, and pools, and at Picton Castle mount and summerhouse were combined. Another example is the stepped mount which survives next to the private chapel of Gwydir Uchaf House (Gwynedd), which was probably part of its garden layout.

*A vignette of the old house at Rug, Clwyd, 1791, showing the garden mount (By permission of Gwynedd County Record Office).*

There is evidence for the reusing of earlier mounds such as Bronze Age burial mounds and medieval mottes in a few gardens. The summerhouse at Rhiwperra sat on a probable motte. At Erddig, Badeslade's engraving of 1740 shows that the Norman castle motte at the northern end of the grounds was incorporated into the ornamental layout. It had a circular building, possibly a summerhouse, on top. The mound at Rug (Clwyd) began life as a Bronze Age burial mound, was enlarged for use as a motte by the Normans, and then was 'adorn'd for an ornamᵗ...' in the garden. Thus it was recorded by the Reverend John Lloyd in a letter of 1693 to Edward Lhuyd, the great antiquary, who was on the look-out for what he called 'observables', which included 'any odd thing, as toads & c. in stone, any old thing in Turfpits'. A drawing of 1791 shows the mount standing next to the old house (which was demolished in about 1800) with a walk round it and a flagpole on top.

# Chapter 4
# *Gardening as Landscape Painting: 1730 to 1830*

*Paxton's Tower, Dyfed, built in 1815 as an adornment to the park of Middleton Hall (By courtesy of the Wales Tourist Board).*

The century from the early 1700s to the early 1800s saw the most dramatic changes in Welsh gardens and parks. During the reigns of Queen Anne and George I, from 1702 to 1727, a revolutionary change in thinking about 'Nature' took place in intellectual circles in London. 'Nature', as depicted in the paintings of French artists such as Poussin and Claude Lorraine, and as written about by Roman writers such as Virgil and Pliny, was equated with goodness and beauty, and became the orthodox setting for great houses. The architectural style thought suitable to accompany such landscapes was Palladian. Everything was to be bold and stately, with no 'crimping, diminutive, and wretched Performances'.

Perhaps the most dramatic new thinking was that it was now desirable to see the park and countryside from the house, and conversely for the house to be seen in its grand setting. To achieve this garden walls were pulled down and replaced by sunk fences, or ha-has. From tentative beginnings in the 1730s this new expansiveness, with 'the

Beauties of Nature elegantly dress'd and Adorn'd', led to the banishment of 'Knots or Flourishes', the removal of flowers and vegetables to a distant, hidden walled garden, the sweeping away of formal features such as avenues and canals, and the surrounding of mansions by lawns, groves, and parks featuring such 'natural' elements as sinuous lakes, clumps of trees and gentle grass slopes. The culmination of this trend was seen in the landscaping of 'Capability' Brown (see pp. 45-6) from the 1750s to the 1770s.

Various factors delayed the appearance of this new style in Wales. The first half of the eighteenth century was a difficult time for landowning families, and debt led to the abandonment, amalgamation, or reduction to farmhouses of numerous smaller properties. Many of the greater families declined or even disappeared as a result of a lack of male heirs or catastrophic debts. Through marriage and purchase, land was concentrated into the hands of fewer families, some of whom were incoming English or Scottish. This led to much absentee ownership which was not conducive to innovations in landscaping. That the 'old style' was still in existence on many estates in the later eighteenth century is shown by the formal features on estate maps of the time.

However, new-found wealth, often from mineral exploitation or commercial enterprise, led to a renewed burst of estate improvement from the 1770s onwards. Turnpike roads, built after about 1760, made travel to town houses in London and Bath easier, and metropolitan values, as promulgated by gentlemen's magazines, were gradually adopted. Welsh values gave way to a more cosmopolitan taste and connoisseurship, and landscaping in Wales finally became popular in the 1770s. Before that there were a few isolated innovators.

## 'Rural Gard'ning': Leeswood

The choked lake, tangled woodland and giant yews of Leeswood (Clwyd) today give little clue to the way the park was first laid out for George Wynne by Stephen Switzer, between 1728 and 1732. Switzer took some of the first practical steps in opening up views, and laying out rural and extensive gardens – as he called them – but his layouts were still of a transitional nature, with informality firmly encased in a geometric framework. Very little of Switzer's landscaping work survives elsewhere, so Leeswood remains a very important relic of a little known era. Most of the planting has gone, and the clipped yews are now giant trees, but most of the earthworks of the garden survive, and Leeswood possesses Wales's earliest ha-has.

Switzer was called in to Leeswood by a man who had just made a fortune (all too short-lived) from exploiting a lead mine on Halkyn Mountain nearby. Wynne was a man of taste. He had connections with Lord Burlington, whose innovations were leading the way in architecture and landscaping in England, and he sponsored the great Welsh landscape painter Richard Wilson (1714-82) to travel in Italy between 1750 and 1756.

To go with Wynne's vast new baroque mansion (now greatly reduced), reputedly designed by Francis Smith of Warwickshire at a cost of £40,000, Switzer laid out a large area to the north and east as an extensive garden, with woodland cut through by intersecting rides flanked by yews and terminating in pavilions, circular pools (later amalgamated into a lake), a bowling green, a large circular mount and a small earthwork amphitheatre. Closing the main axis in front of the house is the great gatescreen, the 'White Gates', probably made in about 1726 by Robert Bakewell of Derbyshire. The gate screen is topped by two lead sphinxes, and was originally flanked by small pavilions, now by the later entrance on the Mold road. The 'Black Gates', originally on the lane to the west of the house, at the end of the main cross axis, have been moved three times and have ended up at the entrance to Tower, a few miles away. The garden was embellished with obelisks, a statue, a sundial, and stone chairs and a table on the bowling green. Two chairs and the table now stand rather drunkenly on top of the mount, witnesses to two hundred and sixty years of gradual change.

## 'A Domain of Parkish Ground': The Gnoll

If lead produced the means to create Leeswood, copper and coal provided them for The Gnoll. Another early garden innovator in Wales was the industrialist Herbert Mackworth, whose father had acquired The Gnoll, Neath (W. Glamorgan), through marriage. A very wealthy and enterprising man, he succeeded his father in 1727, and combined use and pleasure by damming streams above the house into a series of ponds. The head of water was used to drive machinery in his mines and copper smelting works below, while around and above the ponds the grounds were landscaped in the 1740s with paths, planting of pines and spruces, and a long artificial cascade at the head of the largest pond. At the foot of the cascade, which descended in stages built up with drystone walling, were an arched bridge and a root house, with an artificial cave near the top. Several late eighteenth-century visitors describe this cascade, which was made more dramatic for onlookers by the release of a body of water from a reservoir. Henry Wyndham wished that art had been more concealed in the making of the channel, and John Byng preferred 'the first, modest and rural fall' to that produced by the release of water. All but the most ephemeral elements of the landscaping at The Gnoll can still be seen, including the later follies (see p. 49).

Important though Leeswood and The Gnoll were, perhaps the most influential landscaping of the middle of the century in Wales took place on the edge of the Wye valley, at Piercefield, near Chepstow, where Valentine Morris created one of Wales's most celebrated eighteenth-century parks (see p. 50).

Above: *Stone seats on top of the mount at Leeswood, Clwyd (Photograph: author).*

Below: *The artificial cascade at The Gnoll, W. Glamorgan (Photograph: author).*

*Nanteos, Dyfed: a Palladian mansion ornamented with a landscape park.*

# Elegant Seats, Rich Groves and Smiling Lawns

Leeswood, The Gnoll and Piercefield, despite their individual importance, had little contemporary impact on landscaping in Wales as a whole. Although a few Palladian houses were built, such as Nanteos (Dyfed) in 1739, and Wynnstay in 1736-39, and some older houses, such as Taliaris (Dyfed) were remodelled in classical style in the first half of the eighteenth century, it appears that initially there was little attempt to give them the classic Palladian treatment of grass slope down to winding lake.

The late start to Welsh landscaping meant that the style adopted initially was a version of Capability Brown's, with 'elegant seats' set in parks of 'rich groves and smiling lawns'. John Byng gave satirical instructions on the making of such parks in 1787, which began: 'If you should have purchased a good OLD FAMILY HALL, seated low and warm, encircled by woods, and near a running stream, pull it down...'. There are further instructions to place the house in a prominent position, cut down all trees near it, grub up all hedges, and make the approach as meandering as possible. He continues: 'in place of the nasty decaying old oaks, you may PLANT, either single or in clumps, the larch, and Scotch Fir, or the Lombardy poplar. If there are any old formal AVENUES, cut them quite down, and leave not one tree standing to disgrace your taste'. He then advocates a shrubbery, benches with Latin mottoes, temples 'dedicated to the *Heathen Gods*, and 'numberless' ha-has. Sheep, peacocks and guinea fowl complete the scene.

This, in essence, is the sort of park that the Georgian gentry made all over lowland Wales. Hedges were grubbed up and public roads rerouted round the parks. At Llannerch, Samuel Johnson, visiting in 1774, mourned an avenue of oaks cut down 'in a foolish compliance with the present mode'. The terraces of Powis Castle had a narrow escape (see p. 31), and a visitor in 1777 remarked that 'a common Undertaker in Taste, would immediately convert the clipt hedges and true-love-knots, into a gaudy and unmeaning shrubbery'. At Pontypool Park, seat of Capel Hanbury Leigh in the early nineteenth century, the canal and parterres were still there when William Coxe visited in about 1800, but 'these specimens of false taste will soon be removed' he said, and they were.

Visitors to Wales between about 1770 and 1820 testified to the spread of landscape parks, however watered down, to many gentlemen's seats.

The designers of most are unknown, and were probably owners in conjunction with their agents and gardeners. There seem to have been very few Welsh landscape gardeners. John Evans was an assistant of Capability Brown, and worked at Wynnstay (see p. 46), and in 1817 and 1818 Charles Price of Llechryd (Dyfed) was advertising his services in the local papers:

*40 years experience in the profession. furnishes designs to form and improve parks, pleasure grounds, pieces of water. References from respectable families given...*

Most parks were middling to small in size, like Penpont, near Brecon, whose 'finely clumped' park was much admired. Some of the earliest larches in Wales were planted here and at neighbouring Abercamlais before 1743, and a venerable specimen remains on the Penpont lawn. Fine parks were made to complement new villas, such as Merthyr Mawr (W. Glamorgan), designed in 1806-8 by Henry Wood for Sir John Nicholl, or Coed Coch (Clwyd), begun in 1804 and designed by Henry Hakewill. The antiquary Richard Fenton was scathing about the tastelessness of some: 'a few formal clumps disposed so as to admit a glimpse of a distant horsepond, the ruins of a windmill, a kennel in the mask of a church, and bits of Gothic injudiciously stuck here and there...'. At Nanteos, one of the most interesting features of the park is an eye-catcher – a dog kennel disguised as a temple! However, contemporary visitors admired many tasteful lawns and groves, and hot-houses were mentioned approvingly.

The rolling, well-wooded landscape of lowland Wales lent itself to this kind of park, and it was said that all the discerning owner had to do was position his house correctly to have a ready-made landscape park around him. Some houses, like Baron Hill and Plas Newydd on Anglesey, were already in superb positions. Others, like Trawscoed (Dyfed), which was 'set down in an obscure corner of the park', Golden Grove (Dyfed), Margam Abbey and Clytha (Gwent), were not, and some owners built new houses in 'better' positions. On many estates large-scale tree planting, both commercial and ornamental, took place. At Golden Grove, trees in the park in 1781 included Weymouth pine, spruce, silver fir, larch, lime, cedar of Lebanon, Spanish chestnut and beech. It seems that there was little earth moving except for the smoothing of lawns around the house, and not many artificial lakes were made. Views of Wales's beautiful rivers or coastline provided the watery element in many parks.

# 'Et in Arcadia ego': Pembrokeshire and the Tywi Valley

The scenery of parts of Wales was so like a landscape park anyway that some particularly fine examples were made with little effort. The inner reaches of Milford Haven in Pembrokeshire, Swansea Bay (W. Glamorgan), which was likened to the Bay of Naples, the Tywi valley (Dyfed), and the

*At Plas Newydd, Anglesey, the gardens were landscaped by Humphry Repton at the end of the eighteenth century (By courtesy of the Wales Tourist Board).*

*Picton Castle, Dyfed, landscaped from the late 1770s onwards (Photograph: author).*

*Dinefwr Park: Capability Brown's first commission in Wales. He visited in 1775, and added large clumps of beech trees on the hill above Llandeilo (National Trust Photographic Library / Jenny Hunt).*

*Dinefwr Park and Castle, Dyfed, drawn by Mrs Jane Mary Oglander and her niece, Frances Dorothea, in about 1804 (By courtesy of the National Library of Wales).*

Menai Strait (Gwynedd) were all singled out by visitors as exceptionally beautiful areas.

Gentlemen's seats are particularly thick on the ground on the upper reaches of Milford Haven, and the adjoining parks of Picton Castle and Slebech stand out as very fine. Picton Castle is medieval in origin, continuously occupied since the late thirteenth century, for most of that time by the Philipps family. Lord Milford made many improvements from the late 1770s onwards, including the making of a 'romantic' walk through the wood leading down to the river, with frequent seats and a hermitage. The earlier avenue and mount were retained, but Lord Milford may have rebuilt the summerhouse which stood on the mount as a 'handsome' belvedere. There are still 'romantic' walks through the woods, although much of the planting dates from after the eighteenth century, and hidden in the woods between Picton and Slebech is the small hermitage.

North-east of Picton is Slebech, originally a commandery of the knights of St John of Jerusalem, the ruins of whose chapel (subsequently the parish church until 1850) stand near the house. From 1546 to 1757 it was the home of the Barlow family, but in 1773 it came to John Symmons by marriage; he rebuilt 'castle-wise', possibly using Anthony Keck as his architect. Symmons's improvements to house and grounds of about 1776 were so expensive that he had to sell in 1783. The park was well wooded, miles of carriage drive were made, and there is a possibility that some unusual landscaping was undertaken by mounding up and planting with trees two tidal islets in the estuary in front of the house. Happily, the old terraces were not destroyed in the landscaping. In 1792 George Currie, the agent, wrote from Slebech to the owner Nathaniel Phillips to ask what trees he should order for the walls. A fortnight later he threw a familiar light on park and garden management when he wrote that 'Lord Milford's deer... begins to be troublesome. Some of them has been out and in that garden below the hothouse. They come across the canal'.

On the other side of the estuary was Lawrenny, then one of the finest houses in Pembrokeshire. Now all is gone, even a later house. But in the 1790s there was a 'smiling lawn variegated with plantations' in front of the house, with magnificent views across the estuary and down the Carew river to Carew Castle.

eight-arch bridge, the grandest eye-catcher in Wales. In 1810 there were numerous young plantations in the park, with deer, a conservatory, pleasure grounds, and a shrubbery, beyond which was a hidden kitchen garden with hot-houses 'on an immense scale'. On the other side of the lake are a grotto and adjoining rustic arch, both built of volcanic lava. Despite the demolition of the house some of the magic remains, and the view of the lake and bridge from the terrace is still a very beautiful one.

Several large landscape parks, notably Golden Grove, Middleton and Dinefwr, were made in the Tywi valley. The attractive landscape of the valley was celebrated by the famous 'Augustan' poet

*In the major landscape park of the late eighteenth century at Stackpole Court, Dyfed, the large lake was retained behind a dam, cunningly concealed behind an arched bridge (Photograph: author).*

Not far away, south of Pembroke, was the other major landscape park of Pembrokeshire, Stackpole Court. The estate had passed by marriage to Sir Alexander Campbell of Cawdor Castle, Moray, in 1698. Here is another case of large-scale works funded by mineral wealth, in this case lead. A new house was built in the 1730s, and letters from the bailiff to Pryse Campbell indicate that there was already a flourishing garden producing grapes and other fruit. On 5 September 1736 he wrote that 'Mr Row of St Petrox and his wife came to take a walk in the garden and to eat some fruit. I gave them a peach that measured ten inches round'. Most of the landscaping was done in the late eighteenth century by Lord Cawdor. It was on a grand scale, with a long terrace in front of the house overlooking a 'deep romantic' valley in which a large lake was made, with a dam cunningly hidden by a magnificent

James Dyer (1699-1757) in his poem 'Grongar Hill' (1726). Dyer's home was the nearby Aberglasney, whose enigmatic arcaded gardens, with a raised walk around three sides of a garden enclosure are difficult to date. Although ancient in appearance, they are not mentioned until 1793. If earlier, the most likely builder would have been a member of the Rudd family which owned the house during the seventeenth century.

At Golden Grove extensive improvements were made for John Vaughan in the 1780s, including much tree planting. In 1781 thousands of saplings of trees such as Weymouth pine, silver fir, larch, lime, spruce, cedar of Lebanon (24), Spanish chestnut, beech and oak were bought for the park from Kensington nurseries. After 1790 further trees and seeds were bought for the garden and conservatories. In 1788 the architect John Nash was paid ten guineas for designing a cold water bath. But this fine house was demolished, and the new gardens abandoned in 1826, and a new house, designed for Lord Cawdor by Sir Jeffrey Wyatville, was completed in 1832 in a more prominent position.

The story of Middleton Hall is one of the more bizarre chapters in the history of Welsh parks. William Paxton returned from India with a fortune and a zest for up-to-date water management. He bought Middleton in 1789, and built an imposing neo-classical house, designed by S.P. Cockerell, in a prominent position in the middle of the park. It was much admired for its splendour by all contemporary visitors. Paxton's ambition was to turn Middleton into a spa, and although this never came about water management was the dominant theme in the park. Streams were dammed to make a string of lakes, between which were cascades and bridges. Nearby were various spa and bathing buildings, and water was piped all over the park and gardens. Overlooking the whole park, and commanding spectacular views of the Tywi valley, is 'Paxton's Tower', built in 1815, also by Cockerell, to commemorate the deeds of Nelson. It is a large triangular tower with round turrets in each corner and a central turret above, from which to admire the view. Paxton died in 1824, and the bath and spa buildings soon disappeared. In 1931 the house was demolished, and of the park only a little planting, one lake and some of the rather ponderous water

*The artificial waterfall along with other features at Middleton Hall, Dyfed, are remnants of one of the more bizarre chapters in the history of Welsh parks (Photograph: author).*

features, including a cascade, waterfall and the weir, and ruins of some of the spa buildings survive. The utilitarian features of the gardens have fared slightly better. The egg-shaped ice-house set into a hillside is very well preserved, and next to it is the ruined kitchen garden, which is unusual in having double walls and an annexe for herbs.

# Capability Brown in Wales

At the very end of his career, in the late 1770s, the great landscaper Lancelot 'Capability' Brown (1716-83) was summoned to Wales to embellish the grounds of some of its greatest magnates. Dinefwr Park, then called Newton House, home of George Rice, was the first to be 'chastened and polished'. Brown visited in 1775, and did little, finding that 'Nature has been truly bountiful and Art has done no harm'. When William Gilpin visited earlier, in 1770, he had found it picturesque from every angle, with the woods already 'clumped with great beauty'. Scots pines had been planted in 1746 to commemorate the 1745 rebellion. Not only was the landscape beautiful, but there was a ready-made eye-catcher in the form of the ruined Dinefwr Castle. Brown drew up plans for a kitchen garden and garden walls, and the following year for an entrance. His main additions to the landscape were large clumps of beech trees, which still

*Lancelot 'Capability' Brown, 1716-83 (By courtesy of the National Portrait Gallery).*

remain on the hill above Llandeilo. An avenue from house to castle was broken into clumps at some stage in the late eighteenth century, and a walk to the castle is still called 'Brown's Walk'.

In 1776 John, Lord Mountstuart acquired Cardiff Castle and set about a massive programme of improvement. Capability Brown landscaped the walled enclosure. He demolished the cross-wall and buildings in the outer ward, filled in the moat around the motte and grassed the whole thing over. John Byng, who valued the genuinely old, was scathing in 1787 about the result: it had lost its primitive grandeur, and looked like 'a modern attempt of ruins, at a citizens box – The ivy around the old tower, on the keep is cut down, the sides of which are sloped, and mowed: not a tree is planted, but only some small beds of flowers; so altogether it seems to me as only calculated for the town bowling green...'.

The last of Brown's work in Wales was done at the very end of his life, between 1777 and 1783, at Wynnstay, for Sir Watkin Williams Wynn, fourth baronet, patron of the arts, lavish spender, member of the Society of Dilettanti, and owner of the mightiest estate in north Wales. Wynnstay was a huge park on a plateau above the river Dee, and one of the few in Wales that approached the size of the larger English eighteenth-century parks. It had been created in the late seventeenth century, when the name was changed by the Wynns from Watstay to Wynnstay. The house had been enlarged for Sir Watkin's father by Francis Smith in the 1730s, and subsequently; the present house is a mid-nineteenth century replacement after the existing house was destroyed by fire in 1858. Now the park is largely farmland, cut through by the Wrexham by-pass, with only some buildings and monuments as witnesses to its former glory.

This was Brown's most substantial commission in Wales, but it is not certain how much he did here. Certainly the dairy in the form of a Doric temple is his. It is thought that Brown's landscaping work was done to the east of the house, where Byng noted a neat and well laid out shrubbery in 1784, 'the last work of my friend Lancelot Browne'. After Brown's death in 1783 an assistant, John Evans, continued the landscaping until 1785, and it was he who converted the formal canal of the early 1770s into a narrow lake. Of a further lake, now gone, in the lower part of the park, Byng said: 'B's intention was to have form'd a very fine piece of water by means of a great dam; and part of this plan is now advancing, but in a very inferior scale to what Browne proposed'. By the lake was a small shrubbery in which was a large open cold bath, and Evans is credited with designing a cascade of rockwork, long since gone, similar to that at Bowood. An interesting anachronism at the time was the planting of a formal avenue from the house to Ruabon.

Wynnstay is remarkable for its numerous lodges and monuments, on which a succession of eminent architects worked. Following Brown's dairy were the Ruabon gateway and a Doric bath-house, both of which survive. The Doric column (1789), Park Eyton Lodge, and Rhos y Madoc Lodge are by or attributed to James Wyatt, and the strangely Mannerist Newbridge Lodge is by C.R. Cockerell. The Nant-y-Belan Tower, now ruined but in a superb position overlooking the Dee valley, was built before 1812 by Sir Jeffrey Wyatville as a memorial to the fifth baronet's 'Ancient British Fencibles' who fell in the Irish rebellion of 1798. The castellated lodge of Waterloo Tower, possibly by Benjamin Gummow, was built to commemorate the battle.

Beyond these three definite commissions, it is a moot point whether or not Brown designed the park of Wenvoe Castle (S. Glamorgan). Certainly while he was working on Cardiff Castle his son-in-law,

Henry Holland, was designing buildings both at Cardiff and at Wenvoe. Sir Edmund Thomas had vastly overspent on improvements to the grounds in the middle of the century, and his son was forced to sell to the newly wealthy Peter Birt, who rebuilt 'castle-wise' in 1776-77 (the house was demolished in 1910). Thomas's landscaping included the planting of clumps of fir trees, moving roads, and pulling down houses and hedges, but by 1798 the park had a more 'Brownian' appearance, with a sweeping lawn in front of the house, rounded clumps, and one of Wales's very few perimeter belts (a narrow strip of woodland around the edge of the park).

*Detail from a plan of the park at Wenvoe Castle, S. Glamorgan, showing planting and walks (By kind permission of Glamorgan Record Office).*

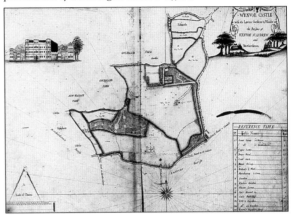

# William Emes in Wales

From the 1760s to the end of the century William Emes of Derbyshire laid out a considerable number of parks in and around Staffordshire. A few of his commissions took him further afield, and at least seven of these were in Wales. Emes worked in the same general style as Brown, but with less assurance and imagination.

His first and biggest project in Wales, and one that took him twenty-four years, was begun in 1764 for Chirk Castle. Major changes were made to both park and gardens. The park was improved by extensive tree planting, both in plantations and clumps, the removal of field boundaries, the closing of public roads, and the making of new curving drives. In the gardens all formality was removed. In 1770, the superb baroque gatescreen (p. 29) was taken down and re-erected at the park entrance (the present exit), Hercules and Mars were banished, and a ha-ha, begun in 1761, was made between garden and park. There was even some earth-moving: the hill in front of the castle was lowered, and the ground between the castle and the old bowling green to the south-east of the castle was sloped. The garden was laid out informally, with a shrubbery in the area now known as the Wild Garden. A 'Green House' (1766-67) by Joseph Turner stood on the site of the Hawk House. The old terrace at the far end of the garden was given a ha-ha instead of a wall, and at the north end a delightful small classical pavilion, then called a 'Retreat Seat', was built in 1767. It is still there.

Much of the structure of the present-day layout at Chirk, but not the planting, is more or less that created by Emes. A few trees in the park, particularly oaks and beeches, date from his landscaping.

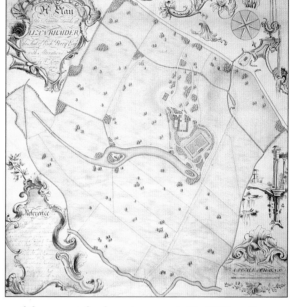

*Part of the plan of Llanrhaeadr Hall, Clwyd, drawn by William Emes, 1771 (By kind permission of Clwyd County Record Office).*

*The landscape park of Chirk Castle, where much of the structure of the present-day layout was created by William Emes, beginning in 1764 (By courtesy of the Wales Tourist Board).*

The 'Cup and Saucer' at Erddig, built in 1774 by William Emes (National Trust Photographic Library / John Bethell).

Between 1767 and 1789 Emes was improving the park at Erddig (see p. 35). John Byng visited in 1781 and thought the woods and meadows 'happily dispos'd'. He continued: 'having peeped into the kitchen garden and pluck'd some currants, we took the round of the wood-walks, and pleasure ground, which are well laid out, and only want gravel, (the want of Wales). The views are good, especially from one point, which commands Wrexham steeple; but the dairy house is out of all character, having never held one bowl of milk; and the stream, whose course has been chang'd to flow under the wood, is paltry, and contemptible. The trees are of a fine growth, and many of a Druidical size'.

Emes also did some work at Powis Castle (see p. 31), and at the Old Rectory at Hawarden (Clwyd) in the 1770s. In 1771 he provided a plan, probably little of which was carried out, for Llanrhaeadr Hall in the Vale of Clwyd, possibly to complement an unexecuted plan by Robert Adam for a grand remodelling of the house. At Baron Hill, Anglesey, in 1776, the seventh viscount Bulkeley began rebuilding his house to a design of Samuel Wyatt. Between 1777 and 1779 Emes redesigned woodland behind the house, and shaped the view across the Menai Strait to 'the Alpine display of the whole extended Snowdonia' with tree planting.

In 1774, Emes was at Gregynog (Powys), working for Arthur Blayney. His plan proposed radical restructuring of the park, with groves, drives and lakes. Some of this was carried out, but much was later obscured, and the lakes, if made, were later filled in. A further commission is mentioned by a late eighteenth-century traveller, who said that the grounds of Mr Price's house, Rhiwlas, at Bala (Gwynedd) were laid out in 'very elegant modern taste under the judicious auspices of Mr Eames'. There was a fine lawn down from the house to the town, and a pleasant winding walk along a 'rapid torrent' in a dell.

In 1776 Emes laid out the grounds of the newly-built Penrice Castle (W. Glamorgan), designed by Anthony Keck for Thomas Mansel Talbot of Margam Abbey. The sloping ground of the park, overlooking Oxwich Bay, was landscaped with artificial lakes, and the view was shaped with planting. At the entrance a 'ruined' castle was built, and to the south-east of the house was a classical greenhouse or orangery. Contemporary visitors found this 'highly-ornamented villa' incongruous in the 'rough' landscape, and the mock ruin at the entrance absurd, with the real one nearby. As Benjamin Heath Malkin said, 'he has given all the elegance of Twickenham to a remote corner'.

Penrice Castle, W. Glamorgan, where William Emes landscaped the grounds in 1776.

Apart from Brown and Emes, the other major figure in landscape design of this period was Humphry Repton, whose work is considered in the next chapter (see pp. 61-2). One or two lesser landscape gardeners, however, are known to have worked in Wales. Adam Mickle, a Yorkshireman, landscaped the park at Tredegar House in 1790. All his suggestions were carried out except the removal of some of the walled gardens and stables. Most of the avenues were removed or broken up, including the main double one up to the Iron Age hillfort, and a new turnpike road was driven through the park to the north of the house. A rather ineffective lake was dug out and surrounded with shrubberies (the towering conifers now around it are Victorian additions). Mickle's other work in Wales, in about 1795, was to design a drive from a new lodge at Piercefield (see p. 51), for Lieutenant-Colonel Mark Wood.

Samuel Lapidge, a former draughtsman of Capability Brown, laid out a small park at Llanarth Court (Gwent) for John Jones in 1792. Working very much in Brown's style, he gave the new house a setting of sweeping lawns and a small, narrow lake, which survives.

# 'Here a Gothic Arch! there a Corinthian Capital!': Ornamental Buildings

**P**arks and gardens of the landscape period were embellished with decorative buildings in various styles, including temples, belvederes, towers, eye-catchers, grottoes, 'dairies', baths, root houses and other constructions of a more or less whimsical nature. One of the more extreme examples in Wales was at Trevecca (Powys), where Howel Harris embellished the grounds of his religious community with 'architectural absurdities... Here a Gothic arch! there a Corinthian capital! Towers, battlements, and bastions!'. More serious in purpose were the two late eighteenth-century forts – Fort Williamsburg (now derelict) and Fort Belan (now lived in) – built at Glynllifon (Gwynedd) by Lord Newborough, from which he planned to defend the country against Napoleon. One of the earliest garden buildings in the Gothic style in Wales is a castellated summerhouse, originally at Llandaff House, Cardiff (S. Glamorgan), and in existence by 1776; it is now in the grounds of Rookwood Hospital, Cardiff. Two delightful Gothic buildings of about 1814 survive at Nerquis Hall (Clwyd). At the west end of the walled garden stands an orangery with cast-iron tracery, designed by Benjamin Gummow, and in a field to the north stands 'Cow Castle', a two-dimensional castellated eye-catcher. At Sketty Park House, near Swansea (W. Glamorgan), there was a stone vaulted Gothic belvedere, built in about 1810, which was modelled on the chapter house at Margam Abbey.

Many ornamental park and garden buildings have long since disappeared, and are only known from maps, paintings or records, such as those at Leeswood, Rhiwperra, Picton Castle, Castle Hall (Dyfed), Middleton Hall, Piercefield and Hafod (Dyfed). Some are reduced to ruins, such as the imposing belvedere at Kilgetty, and the Gothic folly tower at Brynkir (Gwynedd). Castellated towers were popular, perhaps reflecting the ruined medieval castles that abound in Wales. One was built at Downing (Clwyd, restored), home of Thomas Pennant, in 1810, and another on a hilltop at Trevor (Clwyd) in 1827. The tower at Maenan Hall (Gwynedd), which has been restored and has a banqueting room on the upper floor, dates to about 1790. A folly tower was built on the ridge above Pontypool Park by Capel Hanbury in the second half of the eighteenth century. Rebuilt as a tall octagonal tower in 1837 by Capel Hanbury Leigh, it

was demolished in 1940, when it was thought that German aircraft might use it as a marker.

Romanticism is strongly apparent at Soughton Hall, where William Bankes, a friend of the poet Byron, and his architect Sir Charles Barry, chose a supposedly Spanish style for alterations to the house in the late 1820s. In the garden they added 'Spanish' turrets standing on naturalistic rockwork to the corners of the earlier forecourt and garden walls.

Apart from the lodges of Wynnstay, perhaps the most extensive collection of park buildings of the second half of the eighteenth century is at The Gnoll, Neath. Near the top of the cascade is a 'Gothic' castellated facade, and near a walk is a small 'Gothic' arched building. There is a much overgrown alcove grotto behind a terrace near the site of the house, which was used as a sort of museum, housing a collection of ancient relics found on the estate. Two eye-catchers were built in prominent positions outside the park. One, a 'castle', is now gone, but the other, Ivy Tower, remains as an arresting landmark above Neath. Originally used both as an eye-catcher and a banqueting house, it is a large circular Gothic tower, designed by John Johnson, who remodelled the house in 1776 for Sir Herbert Mackworth.

*Clytha Castle, Gwent, built in 1790 as an eyecatcher and summerhouse 'for the purpose of relieving a mind sincerely afflicted by the loss of a most excellent Wife' (Photograph: author).*

A few outstanding buildings were erected in Welsh parks and gardens during this period. Those at Wynnstay, and Paxton's Tower have already been mentioned. Among the most notable, and best preserved, are Clytha Castle and Margam orangery. Clytha Castle is a folly, a sham Gothic castle, which stands on a hilltop in the park at Clytha as an eye-catcher and summerhouse.

# Piercefield

*The late eighteenth-century house at Piercefeld, Gwent, which replaced an earlier house. Piercefield was much visited by Wye valley tourists, drawn by superb views and enchanting walks.*

*Entrance to the Giant's Cave, one of the most dramatic features of the Piercefield walks.*

In the middle of the eighteenth century a few parks in Britain were made in dramatic or 'sublime' landscapes. Piercefield, on the edge of the Wye valley, was one of the most successful. The landscape was dramatic indeed, with the river Wye snaking down to Chepstow between sheer cliffs and steep wooded slopes. The 'dizzy heights and abrupt precipices', the 'impending rocks' and 'hanging woods', contrasted dramatically with the cultivated Lancaut peninsula, surrounded on three sides by the river. This is still an 'enchanting spot, where nature wantons in such variety, and combines so great a portion of the beautiful, the picturesque, and the sublime'.

The park was bought in 1740 by Valentine Morris's father, a plantation, slave and cattle owner in Antigua. Valentine came to live here in about 1752, after his marriage to Mary Mordaunt. The house, predecessor to the present one, was well sited near the edge of the valley, with magnificent views south to the Bristol Channel and beyond. Morris laid out the park in the 1750s with the help of his wife and Richard Owen Cambridge, a Gloucestershire gentleman-poet and man of taste who had earlier tried to buy Piercefield. Two local men, William Knowles and Charles Howells, supervised the work.

The main part of the park was unexceptional,

landscaped in the style of Capability Brown. What made Piercefield so famous were the paths along the lip of the valley, which takes two enormous bends at this point. The main walk, most of which still exists and has been incorporated into the Wye Valley Walk, starts at its southern end on the edge of Chepstow. It is a narrow footpath of gentle gradients, in places cut into the rock, and runs through the woodland on the flank of the valley for about three miles (4.8km) northwards to St Arvans. The walk was punctuated at intervals by features and viewpoints, some of which survive. From the south, first was 'The Alcove', a levelled spur projecting out over the valley, with a stone seat (still there) from which to admire the spectacular view of the lower reaches of the river and Chepstow Castle. Next was 'The Platform', a stone-built viewpoint. The path then crossed the neck of the peninsula, cutting through a small Iron Age hillfort. Within this an alcove-shaped grotto was made, lined with minerals, copper and iron cinders, and rock crystals. The alcove remains but its lining has gone. Around the grotto was a shrubbery, criticized by visitors for being too artificial. On the north side of the great bend, near the house, were the 'Double View', the 'Half-way Seat', a levelled viewpoint, and the 'Druid's Temple', a circle of stones, a few of which remain.

One of the most dramatic moments on the walk was the next feature, the 'Giant's Cave', a tunnel and chamber cut in the cliff face, through which the walk still passes. Over one entrance was a stone giant, now gone, holding a boulder over his head. In 1793 a guidebook lamented that 'his *gigantic majesty* being assailed by a powerful enemy, called *frost,* he soon became divested of his terrific influence, his arms falling off from their joints at the elbows, – in which decrepid and mutilated state he now remains'. Nearby Morris kept some swivel guns. An eighteenth-century visitor who took with him Henry Penruddocke Wyndham's *A Gentleman's Tour through Monmouthshire and Wales* (1781) was advised in an annotation in the book to 'carry some gunpowder and leave it with Mr Morris's gardener in order to fire some small cannon on the Rock as you pass by. The reverberating echo of wch [which] you will find has a wonderful effect'.

North of the Giant's Cave the path split. The main branch, now overgrown, climbed up to the edge of the valley, where it passed 'Lovers' Leap', a viewpoint over a sheer precipice which was originally well railed, and the Temple, a turret with a viewing platform which was demolished in about 1790. A secondary branch of the path (now the Wye Valley Walk) wound down to a grove of oak, beech and sycamore, cleared of underwood, in which there was a 'Cold Bath', now in ruins. For the energetic, a path continued down to the river and then on along it and up to the house by precipitous rock-cut steps. Even by the 1780s these had become almost impassable, and they were soon abandoned.

The climax of the walk was at the north end, where it climbed to its highest point, the Wyndcliff, the view from which in the 1760s was described as 'so sublime that it elevates the mind into instantaneous rapture'. It remains spectacular.

Piercefield soon attracted famous visitors; poets, the Russian ambassador, even John Wesley, were full of praise. Joseph Banks visited for the second time in 1767 and thought it the most beautiful place he had ever seen. But Morris was not to enjoy his walks for long; burdened by massive debt brought on by generosity, idealism, gambling, and the costs of fighting a parliamentary election, he sadly left for the West Indies in 1772, never to return.

In 1785 Piercefield was bought by George Smith, who began a new house to designs by John Soane. He was bankrupt before the roof was on, and Piercefield was bought in 1794 by Lieutenant-Colonel Mark Wood, who finished and extended the house. Wood also made a new drive and lodges, and bounded the park with a high stone wall. He repaired the walks, which continued to be much visited, and which were open to the public on Tuesdays and Fridays. But gradually they fell into disrepair, and were finally closed in the 1850s. In 1923 the park was sold to the Chepstow Racecourse Company, and the racecourse opened in 1926. The house was abandoned, and its forlorn ruins still preside over this most spectacular of 'sublime' landscapes.

Right: *A plan of the grounds at Piercefield, from William Coxe's* An Historical Tour in Monmouthshire *(1801).*

Below: *A miniature of Valentine Morris, who first laid out Piercefield park with its walks in the 1750s (By courtesy of the National Portrait Gallery).*

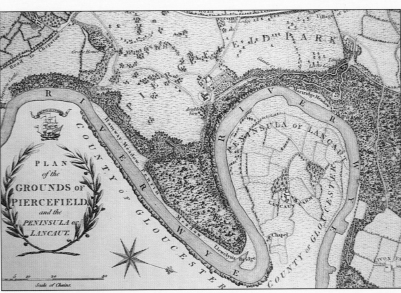

Clytha Castle is largely a two-dimensional fake, with only one solid tower, possibly designed by John Nash, and built for William Jones in 1790 'for the purpose of relieving a mind sincerely afflicted by the loss of a most excellent Wife', as an inscription on the front records. From it there are magnificent views over the park to the Black Mountains. The park was landscaped by Jones in the 1790s, and predates the present house, designed in classical style in the 1820s by Edward Haycock for Jones's nephew, William Jones. At the entrance to the park, Jones built an elegant Gothic arch and screen, also possibly by Nash, which still stand.

*The orangery at Margam, W. Glamorgan, built in 1786-90 to house a famous collection of citrus trees.*

Few orangeries were ever built in Wales, and hence it is of exceptional interest to discover that the longest and grandest example known in Britain is to be found at Margam. This 327 feet (100m) long classical orangery was built by Anthony Keck for Thomas Mansel Talbot between 1786 and 1790 (the terrace in front is a nineteenth-century addition). It stands next to the ruined abbey, and was built to house the famous collection of well over a hundred large citrus trees (see pp. 36-7) in winter. The trees were carried in through an arched entrance at the back, and were heated by hot air from underfloor flues. The pavilion at the east end originally contained Talbot's collection of statuary which he brought back from Italy.

Another orangery is known to have existed at Castle Hall, above Milford Haven (Dyfed). Castle Hall was a 'beautiful villa' first built in about 1770-75 by the nabob John Holwell, who also built the vanished belvedere. In 1804 it was bought by an American Quaker banker, Benjamin Rotch, who greatly improved the house, gardens and grounds. He built terraces, and extensive hothouses and conservatories, including the orangery 'eighty feet long and twenty feet high, entirely of iron and glass, and filled it with the finest orange, lemon and citron-trees. He made pineries too, – three houses, hot, hotter, and hottest – in which three hundred fine large pine-apples were produced in one year'. The orangery is now gone, and the gardens are ruined and abandoned, but this was a showpiece at the beginning of the nineteenth century.

Sculpture was little used in Welsh parks and gardens of this period. Hafod (see p. 58) seems to have had the most. At Llewenny Hall, which Capability Brown visited in 1781, there was a river god and a Sabrina in Coade stone (an artificial stone used for statuary at the time). The porch of Clytha House was ornamented with four Coade stone statues in niches.

# Kitchen Gardens and Ice Houses

As outlined earlier, it was during this period that fruit, flowers and vegetables were banished to walled kitchen gardens away from the house. According to the grandeur of the house these could be anything from about half an acre (0.2ha) to several acres in extent, and sometimes subdivided. The interior would be laid out with perimeter and cross paths, with wall fruit and hot-houses against the walls. There are many in Wales, and a few, such as that at Picton Castle, or that at Cresselly (Dyfed), built in 1776-79 and still in use, are well preserved. But most are ruinous, derelict, or used for other purposes, and the walls are usually all that remain. A few deviate from standard rectilinearity. At Middleton Hall, as well as an unusual double wall there is a curving annexe, thought to have been for herbs. At Clytha the cross paths are serpentine, meeting at a central circular pool.

Before the advent of electricity, ice for the grander establishment was stored in ice-houses. These were brick-lined egg-shaped or rectangular chambers, often underground or built into a hillside. About a hundred are known to survive in parks in Wales. That at Middleton Hall has been mentioned (p. 45), but there are many other well preserved examples, such as at Leeswood, Stouthall (W. Glamorgan), Piercefield, Troy House, and Llanwern Park (Gwent). Bodrhyddan Castle (Clwyd) has a beautiful example, with the ice-cart shed next to it, and at Pontypool Park there is an unusual pair side by side.

# Chapter 5

# The Picturesque and the Romantic in Wales: 1770 to 1830

*The view from the veranda at Rheola, W. Glamorgan, painted by*
*Thomas Hornor, 1817 (By courtesy of the National Library of Wales).*

Towards the end of the eighteenth century a new era began in the appreciation of Welsh landscape. The turnpike roads made access easier; there was a renewed interest in antiquities; the French Revolution and Napoleonic Wars made continental travel difficult; and a reaction set in against the shaven slopes, rounded clumps and serpentining lakes of Brownian landscaping in favour of more intricate, 'distressed' scenery. This was to crystallize into the notion of the Picturesque, and parts of Wales were to play a key role in this new taste in Britain as a whole. Terms such as 'picturesque', 'awful' and 'sublime' had more precise meanings at the time than they do now. 'Picturesque' was applied to the varied and irregular, while 'awful' and 'sublime' implied hugeness and wildness, whether of mountain or waterfall.

As wilder landscapes began to be appreciated, Wales – and in particular Snowdonia and the Wye valley – was gradually discovered. There were a few early pioneers in this taste for the 'awful' and 'sublime'. In 1738 Reverend Thomas Herring, bishop of Bangor, was 'agreeably terrified with something like the rubbish of creation' on his travels in north Wales. Lord Lyttleton of Hagley toured north Wales

in 1756 and thought that the park at Wynnstay should be extended to take in the gorge of the river Dee. Snowdonia was the closest many had come to an 'Alpine' landscape, and the Italianate paintings of Welsh mountains by the Welsh landscape painter Richard Wilson helped project Wales as a land of romantic beauty.

By 1806 Sir Richard Colt Hoare could say that 'Wales has of late years become the fashionable tour of the man of fortune, and the more instructive one of the artist'. He made many journeys in Wales between 1793 and 1810, and frequently rested at his picturesque fishing box, Vachdeiliog (now a motel), on the shore of Lake Bala (Gwynedd). Joseph Cradock in 1776 found one spot near Beddgelert that was 'the noblest specimen of the Finely Horrid, the eye can possibly behold', and commented that 'in the Vale of Clwyd indeed You have the Lively and the Beautiful, but in Montgomeryshire the Awful and Sublime'. Caernarfon was seen as the last outpost of civilization, and returning from Snowdonia was a re-entry into 'Day-light and the polite world'. Tourist accounts proliferated in the 1770s, for (as Cradock noted) 'every one now who has either traversed a steep mountain, or crossed a small channel, must write his Tour'.

*The spectacular view from the Wyndcliffe, looking across a great bend in the river Wye. The Piercefield walks cling precipitously to the cliffs above the river, contrasting with the cultivated fields of the Lancaut peninsula below (By courtesy of the Wales Tourist Board).*

## Nature as a Painter

As early as 1745 the Reverend Dr John Egerton, rector of Ross-on-Wye, organized boat trips down the river Wye, taking in the spectacular scenery between Ross and Chepstow. Valentine Morris began laying out his walks along the top of the valley at Piercefield in the 1750s (see p. 50), and almost immediately they became renowned and much visited. In 1787 it was said of Piercefield that it was 'for ever on an exhibition, and in a glare'. By this time the 'Wye Tour' had been popularized by William Gilpin, who took a boat from Ross to Chepstow in 1770, and published his highly influential *Observations on the River Wye* in 1782. He commented that 'If you have never navigated the Wye you have seen nothing'. Gilpin was looking for what he called 'the Picturesque', or 'that kind of beauty which would look well in a picture'. His rules were precise, with composition, roughness and variety of key importance. He found the valley, with its 'lofty banks' and 'mazey course', ornamented by woods, rocks and buildings, truly picturesque.

The high spot on the Wye Tour was undoubtedly Tintern Abbey. Gilpin himself found it disappointing from a distance, and hemmed in by mean cottages. The abbey was saved from total destruction by the fourth and fifth dukes of Beaufort, who had antiquarian interests. From the mid century stone robbing was stopped and the interior tidied up. Gilpin found the abbey better at close quarters, but he was not above suggesting improvements: 'a number of gabel-ends hurt the eye

*A watercolour of Tintern by Paul Sandby, who was one of the many artists drawn to the abbey by its picturesque qualities (By courtesy of the National Library of Wales).*

with their regularity; and disgust it by the vulgarity of their shape. A mallet judiciusly used... might be of service in fracturing some of them...'! John Byng liked the ivy, choughs and jackdaws, and was impressed by its 'awfull grandeur', but disliked the well mown floor. 'The way to enjoy Tintern Abbey properly...' he said, 'is to bring wines, cold meat, with corn for the horses... Spread your table in the ruins; and possibly a Welsh harper may be procured from Chepstow'. Tintern had many famous visitors; in the 1790s Turner painted it, Coleridge visited, and Wordsworth wrote of the 'wild secluded scene' in *Lines Written a Few Miles above Tintern Abbey*. The landscape designer Humphry Repton and Uvedale Price, one of the main codifiers of picturesque theory, also took the Wye Tour in this decade.

Gilpin continued down the river in 1770 to Piercefield (see p. 50), which he admired: 'The winding of the precipice is the magical secret, by which all these inchanting scenes are produced'. But the views he called romantic, not picturesque, as he thought them seen from too high.

Gilpin continued down the river in 1770 to Piercefield (see p. 50)

*Illustration by Thomas Rowlandson for William Coombe's satirical book,* The Tour of Doctor Syntax in Search of the Picturesque, *1809 (By courtesy of the Library, University of York).*

The most famous manifestation of picturesque taste in Wales is that created towards the end of the eighteenth century at Hafod by Thomas Johnes (see p. 58). But there were many lesser expressions of this new taste for the sublime, picturesque and romantic. One was Cwm Elan (Powys), later drowned by the flooding of the Elan valley for a reservoir in about 1910. In the 1790s 'the striking

at Hafod by Thomas Johnes (see p. 58)

example of Mr Johnes, has induced Mr Grove to build a house, and form an ornamented territory, with considerable taste, in one of these deserts, which he prefers to his fine seat in Wiltshire'. Cwm Elan was less than twenty miles (32km) from Hafod, and the owner was a cousin of the romantic poet Shelley, who sometimes stayed there. Thomas Jones, a landscape painter who spent much time in Italy, returned to his home of Pencerrig (Powys) in 1787, and in the 1790s proceeded to landscape his park. His most important contribution was a six-acre (2.4ha) lake with an artificial island.

Richard Fenton created a 'Paradise of Landscape' at Plas Glynamel (Dyfed). The situation, above the River Gwaun, was already picturesque, and his planting was lavish. Among other things, he was a plantsman, and specialized in half-hardy plants, including the 'Mexican Aloe', the 'Indian Hymalayan Bamboo', figs, oranges and eucalyptus trees grown out in the open. Towards the end of the garden was a natural cave, which Fenton liked to think had been a cell of St Dubricius.

Picturesque walks and gardens sprang up in the more prosperous Georgian towns of Wales like Brecon (Powys) and Monmouth (Gwent). In Brecon, Priory Walk led from the town into the meadows and to a tea-drinking house. In Monmouth John Tibbs, landlord of the Beaufort Arms, laid out what was described in 1804 as a *ferme ornée*. It had a public mall, tea garden and bowling green on an area of meadow below the town called Vauxhall. Until about 1830 it was reached by a rustic wooden bridge. Although these features have long since gone, the Round House on the Kymin hill above the town remains as a testament to the taste for the picturesque. This is a two-storey belvedere erected by the Monmouth Picnic Club in 1794. A winding path led up to it from the town. Here the public could, on payment of sixpence, use the banqueting room and admire the still magnificent views from five windows. There were instructions on how to look at each view in the correctly picturesque manner. Walks were cut

*The Round House on the Kymin, above Monmouth, from whose windows there are magnificent views (Photograph by Wilma Allan).*

along them were six seats, each with a special view created by tying back branches of trees. Next to the Round House the Naval Temple, a small square classical building, was erected in 1800 to commemorate the great early naval battles of the Napoleonic Wars. In 1802 it was visited by Nelson and the Hamiltons.

A spectacular waterfall in Clwyd, Pistyll Rhaeadr, was given picturesque treatment in the late eighteenth century. First, the vicar of Llanrhaeadr-ym-Mochnant, Dr William Worthington, who had already built sham ruins (now gone) above the church, built a cottage near the waterfall 'for tea drinking'. Then Sir Watkin Williams Wynn, fifth baronet, built a rustic pavilion with a tree-trunk portico at the foot of the falls, which were 'improved' by the rebuilding of a natural rock arch. The pavilion is now a cafe.

# 'Animated Prospects': Castles and Abbeys

Just as many of the Welsh gentry were rejecting their history and architectural heritage others were discovering it. For some houses, like Margam Abbey, where the Tudor house was demolished in the 1780s, the discovery came too late. The irony at Margam was that forty years later a brand new house was built in Elizabethan Gothic style.

However, the new appreciation of the ruins of Tintern Abbey led the way for other medieval ruins to be valued, and sometimes used in picturesque schemes. Llandaff Cathedral (S. Glamorgan) was described in 1774 as a 'very picturesque gothic ruin'; Dolbadarn Castle (Gwynedd), commanding the entrance to the Llanberis Pass, and Cilgerran Castle (Dyfed), in a spectacular position above the river Teifi, were much admired and painted. The juxtaposition of 'modern' smelting works and medieval ruins at Neath Abbey (W. Glamorgan) was thought 'sublime'. A terrace walk was made around Abergavenny Castle (Gwent) in about 1800. In 1781 John Byng said of Valle Crucis Abbey, that Sir Watkin Williams Wynn, fourth baronet, 'has built a green and white summer house, at the end of a spruce fishing canal; and from this well-fancy'd retreat, the abbey is conceal'd by the apple trees in a cabbage garden. What charming elegance! How worthy of Clapham or Hackney!!!'. He thought that if the abbey were 'properly embellish'd it would form one of the most delightfully romantic spots in the world: surely Browne never saw this place, or he wou'd have gone wild to have handled it'.

He also had recommendations for Castell Coch (S. Glamorgan): 'the path and around it, might be made pleasant and safe, by a man with a spade, and mattock, in a few days. – In one old bastion, which is guarded from weather, and commands charming views down the river, and to the sea, might be easily fitted up a room, to dine, to drink tea in; and then what a sweet place wou'd it be, for a party to come to from Cardiff Castle'.

The poet Walter Savage Landor started a scheme at the ruined priory of Llanthony (Gwent) which was very similar in aims to Johnes's at Hafod. He wanted to combine beautifying the landscape with profitable farming. However, the intransigence of his tenants, combined with his lavish spending and impetuosity, led rapidly to bankruptcy. Between 1808 and 1813 he spent nearly £70,000 on the estate, building a new house at Siarpal in a picturesque position above the priory, planting hundreds of thousands of trees, including unsuitable cedars of Lebanon, which did not survive, and building bridges and field boundaries. Some of these features remain, but the house is ruined, and of his plantings only some beech, larch and sweet chestnut trees survive to enhance the romantic and picturesque setting of the priory.

*Sir William Watkins Wynn's summerhouse at Valle Crucis Abbey, Clwyd (Photograph: author).*

At Laugharne Castle (Dyfed) the owner, Richard Isaac Starke, made a garden of picturesque shrubberies and lawns in the outer ward, next to his newly built house. A raised walk, later embellished with a summerhouse (known to have been used by Dylan Thomas), overlooked the Taf estuary. Some contemporary visitors found this juxtaposition of genuine ruined castle and artificial garden incongruous; one complained that 'Not only the area, but even one of the towers, is converted to the purposes of horticulture, and filled with the

*A watercolour of the picturesque landmark of Castell Dinas Brân which could be seen from the garden at Plas Newydd (By courtesy of Glyndŵr District Council).*

incongruous ornaments of evergreens and flowering shrubs'. Some of the trees, and most of the layout of the garden in the outer ward, with its winding paths of crushed sea shells, survive, and the whole is soon to be recreated.

Genuine ruins abound in Wales, and some were useful as picturesque landmarks for a park or garden. Dinefwr Castle has already been mentioned (p. 38), and Beaumaris Castle, on Anglesey, embellished the view from Baron Hill. Castell Dinas Brân (Clwyd), perched high up above Llangollen was the distant focus of the view from the garden of Plas Newydd (see p. 60). Some were much closer at hand. At Penrice Castle (see p. 48) the old stronghold stretches up the hill behind the new house, and a summerhouse and aviary were made in it when the park was landscaped. The juxtaposition of old castle with new was nowhere more apparent than at Hawarden (Clwyd), where Sir Stephen Glynne rebuilt the old Broadlane Hall as a castellated mansion, designed by Thomas Cundy, in 1809-10, and rechristened it Hawarden Castle. In the grounds stood the ruined real castle, which Sir Stephen made more picturesque by the addition of an irregular skyline of stone-faced brickwork. Much older is the Neolithic chambered tomb in the grounds of Plas Newydd, which was 'rediscovered' at this time.

Fashionable antiquarianism led to some bizarre inclusions in parks and gardens. If antiquities were lacking they could be supplied. At Baron Hill, Lord Bulkeley built a temple in which he placed the coffin of Princess Joan, daughter of King John and wife of Llywelyn the Great, brought from Llanfaes Priory. A megalithic 'cromlech' was built at Glynllifon. Circles of upright stones, known then as 'druid temples' were placed in some parks, such as Piercefield, and one was planned but not built at Hafod.

*Two drawings by Sir Richard Colt Hoare, 1810: the chambered tomb at Plas Newydd, Anglesey, Gwynedd [above]; and [right] the tomb of Princess Joan at Baron Hill, Anglesey. Both were treated as garden features (By courtesy of the National Library of Wales).*

# Hafod

*Hafod, painted by John 'Warwick' Smith in 1792. In their heyday, both house and grounds were one of the wonders of Wales: 'a paradise in a profound desert' (By courtesy of the National Library of Wales).*

In their prime, the house and grounds of Hafod, in the Ystwyth valley, were one of the wonders of Wales. The very unexpectedness of a highly embellished park in a barren treeless landscape added to the delight and wonder of visitors. It was called 'a second Paradise rising from a newly-subsided chaos', and a paradise in a 'profound desert'. With much of the estate now covered with coniferous plantations it requires some imagination to picture this paradise of two hundred years ago.

Thomas Johnes, scholar, agricultural improver, and idealist, was already familiar with the Picturesque, partly through his cousin Richard Payne Knight, who took a keen interest in the design of the Hafod grounds. Johnes moved to Hafod from Croft Castle, Herefordshire, in the 1780s, and built a Gothic mansion, designed by the Bath architect Thomas Baldwin, above the river. It was later extended by Nash and Johnes, was burnt down in 1807 and rebuilt, again by Baldwin. It had a conservatory 160 feet (49m) long at the end of which was a Neptune fountain by Thomas Banks. Many rare exotics from all over the world were cultivated here.

Johnes's landscaping followed picturesque principles, creating a series of pictures using the simplest of materials and altering as little as possible. His acknowledged mentors were William Gilpin (see p. 54) and William Mason, who described just such a landscape as Hafod in his poem *The English Garden* (1772-81). Gilpin never visited Hafod, but judged it truly pictuesque from Johnes's description and paintings by Thomas Jones. One visitor said of the natural meadow in front of the house: 'No *Brownonian* attempts have been made to slope and swell it', and Johnes himself said of the landscape that 'I have neither shorn or tormented it'. The secret of Johnes's success was his sensitive handling of the beautiful and varied natural scenery. Two carefully planned circuit walks were made around the estate, the longer for men, the shorter for women. These paths, sometimes rock-cut, wound over the hilly ground, sometimes passing 'romantically... by the side of a brawling torrent'. They took in several features such as a simple cold bath, a mill site and nearby cascade, Mrs Johnes's garden, a waterfall viewed from a tunnel cut in the rock (a scene of 'awful sublimity'), and several rustic bridges, sometimes just planks, over the Ystwyth and its tributaries. The 'hand of art' made little appearance.

There were two flower gardens hidden in this picturesque paradise. The idea for them seems to have come straight out of Mason's poem, *The English Garden*, in which he describes flowery glades 'So fragrant, so sequester'd' set in woodland. The first was Mrs Johnes's Flower Garden, a walled enclosure in the valley bottom, which was begun in the mid 1780s. A visitor described it: a 'gaudy flower garden, with its wreathing and fragrant plats bordered by shaven turf, with a smooth gravel walk carried round, is dropped, like an ornamental gem, among wild and towering rocks, in the very heart of boundless woods'. Some found it too artificial. In about 1793 it was given Coade stone arched entrances, and by 1794 contained a Doric temple 'from a design in Stuart's Athens'. There were further Coade stone sculptures including a Triton and possibly a Flora. As time went on the garden was increasingly planted with peat- and shade-loving shrubs, many of American origin. It is of historical importance as perhaps the first 'American' garden in Wales. Now all planting has gone, and only its reconstructed perimeter wall and entrances survive.

The second garden was a private one belonging to Johnes's young daughter Mariamne, a keen botanist. It was a small enclosure on steeply sloping high ground, designed and planted for Mariamne in 1795-96. Its creator, the Scottish agriculturalist Dr James Anderson, divided it into five distinct areas, each for different kinds of plants, in particular alpines. There was also a moss house and a marble urn commemorating Mariamne's pet robin. Just below this secret garden, only the bones of which survive, is a neo-classical obelisk in a prominent position overlooking the valley. It was erected in 1805 to commemorate another agricultural improver, the fifth duke of Bedford, and remains the most prominent landmark at Hafod.

Afforestation played a key role in Johnes's transformations, and millions of trees, including larch, oak, beech, birch, alder, ash, rowan and elm, were raised and planted on the bare hillsides. Larch became predominant after 1798. Johnes's forester, John Greenshields, was Scottish, as was his head gardener James Todd, who had been an assistant gardener at the Botanic Garden in Edinburgh.

Beyond the grounds are further reminders of this era. The rustic arch, designed in 1806 by George Cumberland, was erected by Johnes over the Devil's Bridge to Cwmystwyth road in 1809. He also built The Hafod Arms at Devil's Bridge to accommodate the increasing number of tourists who

Top: *The waterfall at Devil's Bridge gives a good idea of the dramatic scenery at Hafod.*
Bottom: *The duke of Bedford's obelisk, erected in 1805, which remains a prominent landmark at Hafod (Photograph: author).*

came to Hafod (tickets for tours obtainable from the landlord), and the picturesque walks to the Falls of Mynach were laid out in the late eighteenth century.

The tragedy of Mariamne's premature death in 1811, and Johnes's financial ruin led him to leave Hafod soon afterwards. Its heyday was over. Now, apart from the enduring natural beauty of the valley, the main clues to this lost era are the numerous contemporary views, including paintings by J. M. Turner and John 'Warwick' Smith. The house is reduced to a pile of stonework, and the paths are overgrown. Only the walls remain of the great kitchen garden, where Johnes's visitors were surprised to find a pet cockatoo, and most of the built structures have gone or are ruinous. But the natural beauty of the valley remains; the paradise has not entirely disappeared.

# 'This Delicious Solitude': The Romantic Garden

In 1778 two young intellectual Irishwomen, Eleanor Butler and Sarah Ponsonby, ran away together from their straight-laced homes in Ireland, and in 1780 rented Plas Newydd, above Llangollen, together with four acres (1.6ha) of farmland. Over the next fifty years these 'enchantresses', their 'romantic friendship', their 'system', their intense sensibility, and their garden, were to become legendary. Famous visitors, included Wordsworth, Southey, Shelley, the duke of Wellington, Dr Darwin and his son Charles, Sir Walter Scott, and Sheridan. Despite their poverty they moved in elevated local circles, and were particularly friendly

*A font from Valle Crucis Abbey, placed in a shaded spot in the romantic gardens at Plas Newydd, Clwyd (Photograph: author).*

with the Piozzis (Mrs Piozzi, formerly Mrs Thrale, was a great friend of Samuel Johnson) of Brynbella (Clwyd), for whom they were prepared to break a rule of their 'system' of not spending nights away from Plas Newydd.

They found in the remote little cottage, as it then was, just the 'retirement' they were looking for. The position was romantic in the extreme, with views of Castell Dinas Brân, the Trevor rocks, the Berwyn mountains, and a steep drop below down to the miniature ravine of the river Cufflymen. The 'ladies of Llangollen' as they became known were immersed in the Picturesque and Romantic: their library contained all of William Gilpin's books, at least two copies of Uvedale Price's *An Essay on The Picturesque* (1794), and Rousseau's ideas on 'Nature' were a great inspiration. Their favourite gardening book was C. Hirschfeld's *De l'Art des Jardins* (1779) from whose illustrations they copied rustic bridges to cross the river Cufflymen, and from which they culled inscriptions of romantic sentiments for boards hung on trees.

Between the house and ravine was a sloping lawn, on which they used to read the romantic

poetry of Ossian. Below was a flowering shrubbery in which they sometimes hid from unwanted visitors. Particular favourites were the white lilacs which were good for romantic moonlit walks. Through the shrubbery, past the model dairy, fowl yard, drying green and gardens, wound a gravel path, the 'Home Circuit', which gardeners had constantly to rake. Standards were high and many gardeners were sacked! The house and garden were continually improved. In the 1780s, a stone dairy and new kitchen garden were built with a Gothic arch at the entrance. A new thicket was planted, of 'Lilaks Laburnums, Seringas, White Broom, Weeping Willow, Apple Trees, poplar'. A rustic shed and summerhouse with a library overlooking the valley were built, and workmen were sent to attack the Cufflymen with spades and mattocks as it was thought too formal. By 1791, when they began another new shrubbery, the gardens, which contained a wide range of flowering shrubs and perennials, were much admired.

As time went on Eleanor and Sarah became more interested in wild gardening, and concentrated their efforts on the Cufflymen ravine. By 1799 the river had been reshaped into cascades and pools, a birch avenue planted, and a font from Valle Crucis Abbey placed in a shaded spot in the valley, with a spring running into it, and evocative inscriptions dated 1782 on either side. Moss and ferns were encouraged to envelop it. By 1800 the gardens were virtually complete. Nineteenth-century changes, including formal beds and a 'Gorsedd' circle of stones in what had been the field in front of the house, have altered the gardens, and most of the ladies' rustic garden structures have gone. Surrounded as the gardens now are by housing it is hard to imagine the romantic solitude of two hundred years ago.

*A watercolour of the rustic steps in the garden at Plas Newydd (By courtesy of Glyndŵr District Council).*

Nearby, at Brynkinalt (Clwyd), Charlotte, Lady Dungannon, a loyal friend to Eleanor and Sarah, was introducing picturesque features. Between about 1808 and 1814 the park was embellished with a castellated bridge over the river Ceiriog, a cottage of tree trunks and river stones, and a china room and dairy (now demolished).

# Polishing and Trimming the Rocks: Humphry Repton in Wales

Humphry Repton (1752-1818) was the foremost landscaper in England at the end of the eighteenth century. He moved away from Capability Brown's style, and attempted a more practical, pragmatic one, while remaining sensitive to the picturesque qualities of the landscapes with which he dealt. He liked 'agreeable surprise', and brought back formality and terracing around houses. His style is satirized and compared to the Picturesque by Thomas Love Peacock in *Headlong Hall* (1815), which has particular relevance to Wales. Peacock was a friend of the poet Shelley, who in turn was a friend of the builder of the Traeth Mawr embankment (Gwynedd), William Madocks (1773-1828), whose house Tan-yr-allt, near Tremadog, was the first 'Regency' house in north Wales. Madocks bought the estate of Dolmelynllyn (Gwynedd) in the 1790s, built a house, and entertained friends in this wild romantic landscape, which includes the famous Rhaeadr Ddu waterfall, near which one of his friends carved a Latin inscription on a rock. The Shelleys rented Tan-yr-allt in 1812-13, whilst Peacock lived at Maentwrog, nearby. Headlong Hall was a fictitious house near Capel Curig in Snowdonia, and Marmaduke Milestone (Repton) arrived, promising himself the 'glorious achievement of polishing and trimming the rocks of Llanberris'. He found that 'the grounds have never been touched by the finger of taste', and offered to improve them. Later in the visit he attempted to smooth the surroundings of a ruined tower by dynamiting a rocky slope. The real Repton did nothing so drastic in Wales.

Repton had only three definite Welsh commissions, for each of which he produced one of his 'Red Books', which outlined his proposals and contained 'before' and 'after' watercolours to entice owners into agreeing to his schemes. The earliest was in 1793 at Rug (Clwyd), a neo-Grecian house in the upper Dee valley. With admirable restraint, Repton merely added a 'lawn' of fifty acres (20.2ha), remarking that 'the views from the house should aim at comfort and appropriation of landscape, rather than extensive prospect'.

The second commission was a much larger one, for Plas Newydd, on Anglesey, for the earl of Uxbridge. The site is superb, with views out over the Menai Strait to Snowdonia. In the 1780s the grounds were obviously old-fashioned, with 'short steep slopes around the house' and a wall instead of a ha-ha between garden and park. During the 1790s the house was being remodelled in Gothic style by James Wyatt and Joseph Potter, who also bounded the garden below the house with a long terrace, in front of which was a battlemented sea wall complete with bastions, Gothic arches, a jetty and a possible bath-house. Repton first visited in 1798, and the following year he produced recommendations, including a Gothic pavilion modelled on his idea of a monastic chapter house. By 1803 most of his suggestions had been carried out; the woods were filled out to screen the house from the road, the main drive was reorientated, and additional plantings of fir, oak and birch were made. In 1816 the Anglesey Column, the main landmark on the island, was erected. The statue of the famous

Left: *Repton's suggested pavilion (1799) for Plas Newydd, Anglesey (By permission of the British Architectural Library, RIBA, London).* Below: *A portrait of Humphry Repton (By courtesy of the National Portrait Gallery).*

one-legged first marquis of Anglesey was not put on the top until 1860. Although there has been much later planting, and the making of a small Italianate terraced garden in the 1930s, the present layout of lawns, woods and drive, and some of the planting, are Repton's.

Repton's last work in Wales was at Stanage Park (Powys), a commission from Charles Rogers. He visited and produced a Red Book in 1803, and talked of 'The wild and shaggy Genius of Stanedge'. The castellated house, begun in 1803, was partly designed by Humphry and his son John Adey Repton. It was deliberately modelled on Richard Payne Knight's home of Downton Castle, Herefordshire (Payne Knight was one of the main protagonists of the Picturesque style). Repton's work included terraced lawns in front of the house, two picturesque drives, a pond, much tree planting including thousands of larches, and a lodge. The overall result, although masked by later planting, remains visible, and it is still a beautiful, picturesque park.

# John Nash and John Claudius Loudon

The famous architect, John Nash, settled in Carmarthen, and his Welsh architectural work began in the late 1780s. He experimented with many styles, but was influenced by the Picturesque ideas of men such as Uvedale Price, for whom he designed a castle-like Gothic villa, now gone, in Aberystwyth (Dyfed). Of his buildings in Wales very few remain. Some, like Ffynone (Dyfed), have been altered, some, like Rheola (W. Glamorgan), have lost their setting, but the house and estate buildings of Llanaeron (Dyfed) survive. The layout is a planned one, with house, church, cottages and farm buildings all carefully integrated into an intimate arrangement, forming a series of 'pictures' in true picturesque style. At Rheola and Nanteos there is a possibility that Nash and Repton worked in conjunction on the house and grounds respectively. The bones of a modest 'Reptonian' park survive at Derry Ormond (Dyfed), although the neo-classical house, designed by C. R. Cockerell for John Jones and begun in 1824, has been demolished. In front of the house were garden terraces, from which there was a picturesque view across an artificial lake to a folly tower (a Doric column 126 feet – 38.4m – high) on top of a ridge.

John Claudius Loudon, the most eminent authority on gardens in the early nineteenth century, was very influential in their development, although he did little actual landscape designing. His main work in Wales was the alteration of Lapidge's park at Llanarth Court in 1805, with additional planting and a softening of the outline of the lake. Although little now remains, it is likely that he did some landscaping around the fantastic house (now demolished) of Garth (Powys) that he designed for the Reverend Richard Mytton, who had made a fortune in India, in 1811. Both stables and kennels were in the same 'Strawberry Hill' Gothic style as the house. In 1805, Loudon modernized the glasshouses of Hafod, using his invention of an 'inner roofing' or curtain.

*Two paintings of Rheola, W. Glamorgan, by Thomas Hornor, 1817, showing a general view of the grounds [top] and [below], a plan of the estate. The house was the work of the famous architect, John Nash (By courtesy of the National Library of Wales).*

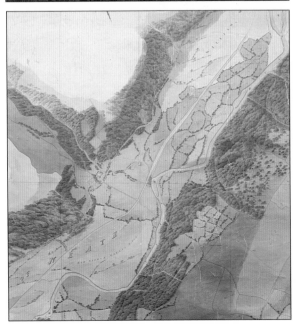

# Chapter 6
# Victorian Parks and Gardens:
# 1830 to 1880

*The fountain centrepiece of the grand terrace at Kinmel Park, Clwyd. The terrace was designed in 'Venetian' style by W. E. Nesfield in 1873, and was intended to complement the new red brick house (Photograph: author).*

Towards the end of the eighteenth century industrial wealth began to grow in Wales, and this trend continued throughout the nineteenth century. Fortunes were made by ironmasters such as the Crawshays of Cyfarthfa Castle (M. Glamorgan), by industrialists such as the Vivians of Singleton Abbey (W. Glamorgan), by quarry owners such as George Pennant of Penrhyn Castle (Gwynedd), and by mine owners such as the Reverend Edward Hughes of Kinmel (Clwyd). The desire for respectability and social standing of these newly rich families, combined with fashionable romanticism, led them to build sham castles and abbeys in Gothic or Elizabethan style. Vast picturesque mansions such as Margam Castle, Cyfarthfa Castle, Singleton Abbey, Talacre Abbey (Clwyd), Woodlands (later Clyne) Castle (W. Glamorgan), Hawarden Castle, Bryn Bras Castle (Gwynedd), Maesllwch Castle (Powys), Hensol Castle (S. Glamorgan), and two Penrhyn Castles were built in the late eighteenth and early nineteenth centuries. The only qualification for emulating Beaumaris, Conwy, Caernarfon or Caerphilly was a deep purse.

Until about 1820 there was more or less a consensus, based on the established principles of good taste, as to how a park or garden should be laid out. The richest employed professionals, the rest copied as best they could. Thereafter the consensus collapsed. Freed from the constraints of 'good taste', aided by new technology, and with a new-found desire for innovation, comfort and artificiality, gardens of all sorts blossomed, and then died or were simplified as fashion moved on and fortunes fell. There are few relics of this colourful era, with its great glasshouses and conservatories, that raised the bedding plants and housed the exotics and pineapples; its colourful beds of half-hardy annuals that filled the gardens; its rock gardens, alpine gardens, heather gardens, wild gardens, woodland gardens, pineta, and Japanese gardens. With the gardens disappeared their proud, and sometimes autocratic, head gardeners, and their small armies of minions. Many of the grandest nineteenth-century houses and gardens, overlarge for modern needs, stand in ruins or have been demolished. Parks have reverted to farmland, their presence marked perhaps by exotic trees such as wellingtonias in the fields, or the odd folly or park lodge. Although there are some splendid survivals, for the most part we are dealing with fragments from a lost world, the entirety of which is difficult to imagine.

# The Victorian Park

Landscape parks continued in existence through the Victorian era in Wales, and older parks had new elements, such as formal gardens round the house, and new planting, grafted on to them. Plant hunters in the Americas and the Far East began to introduce exotic trees and shrubs that were quickly to change the face of the British park and garden. The most important contributions to the landscape were the giant conifers, in particular monkey puzzle (*Araucaria araucana*), Californian redwood (*Sequoia sempervirens)*, wellingtonia (*Sequoiadendron giganteum)* and Japanese cedar (*Cryptomeria japonica)* which were much planted, both singly and in rows and avenues, from the middle of the century onwards. Most Welsh parks and gardens were adorned with these new trees and many giant examples survive to the present day. Leighton Hall (Powys) has a magnificent collection, including an *Abies grandis* which at 184 feet (56m) in 1975 was then the tallest tree in Britain. As well as many other species of conifer, Leighton has the Charles Ackers grove of Californian redwoods, planted by John Naylor in 1858 on the Long Mountain, as seedling trees brought from America in pots, which is now one of the most heavily timbered areas in Europe. Moreover, it was at Leighton that the first Leyland cypress was raised in 1888. It was named after Thomas Leyland, founder of the Leyland and Bullins Bank, whose vast wealth Naylor had inherited. The earliest Leyland cypress was blown down there in 1954. Naylor could not have foreseen that his magnificent forest tree would be planted in so many suburban gardens in the late twentieth century.

Singleton Abbey and Clyne Castle (both now parts of University College Swansea), Margam Castle and Tredegar Park all have good collections of Victorian conifers, and fine avenues of wellingtonias can be seen at Erddig and flanking the former drive of Llantilio Court (Gwent, now demolished).

One of the Welsh parks most praised for its trees in the nineteenth century was Llanover Park, home of Sir Benjamin Hall (later Lord Llanover) from the 1820s. Between 1828 and 1839 the architect Thomas Hopper designed Llanover House in Elizabethan style, and well-wooded gardens were laid out around it. Sir William Hooker of Kew advised on the planting, some of which survives. After the middle of the century separate collections of exotic conifers, or pineta, became popular in England, and there are several in Wales. Golden Grove (Dyfed) has a fine pinetum above the house,

*Large conifers became a prominent feature in Victorian parks. This pinetum at Golden Grove, Dyfed, has many venerable specimens planted by Lord Cawdor at the site (By courtesy of the Wales Tourist Board).*

with many venerable specimens planted by Lord Cawdor, and there is another at Gwysaney (Clwyd) planted to the north of the house by Philip Davies-Cooke. At Pontypool Park a large arboretum of mixed coniferous and deciduous trees, the 'American Gardens', was planted in the 1850s by Capel Hanbury Leigh at the north end of the park, and today huge monkey puzzles, wellingtonias, and Californian redwoods tower above the deciduous canopy.

Some parks had great walls thrown up round them, such as Vaynol (Gwynedd), walled in the 1850s by T. Assheton Smith, and Bodelwyddan Castle (Clwyd), walled in 1830-42. With the walls went lodges, many of which survive, even where the house has gone. A particularly delightful one, now separated from its park, is the Golden Lodge at Kinmel Park (Clwyd, see p. 67) built by W. E. Nesfield in 1868, which is ornamented with carvings of sunflowers (as are other Nesfield buildings in the park), some in flowerpots.

Folly building was still popular, although the more whimsical, such as artificial ruins, went out of fashion. One of the most fantastic Victorian follies in Wales is the Gothic Dry Bridge Lodge at Mostyn Hall, probably built in the 1840s, and still lived in.

A carriage drive passes through it and the Mostyn-Whitford road runs under it in a tunnel.

A few entirely new ornamental parks were made, such as that at The Hendre (Gwent), created between 1830 and 1900 for the Rolls family, in a loosely 'picturesque' style. In the 1890s the landscape designer H. E. Milner (1845-1906), son of Edward Milner (see p. 68) laid out a picturesque drive, known as the Three Mile Drive, from a new entrance on the Rockfield road to the house. It was landscaped all the way, with planting, Pulhamite rockwork (artificial rockwork made by Pulham and Son, of Hertfordshire, itself an interesting innovation), a lake and cascade, and openings in the woods giving picturesque views over the park. It would have been used by some of the very earliest motor cars in the country, driven by Lord Llangattock's son, Charles Rolls. A highly picturesque park was made in the 1830s and 1840s by John Dillwyn Llewelyn at Penllergare (W. Glamorgan). Llewelyn's pioneering photographs of the 1840s and 1850s record the park's appearance (which has now been almost completely obliterated), with its two lakes, plantings of conifers, and an artificial cascade of massive rocks which happily survives.

*The recreation of a tropical landscape in an orchid house, built in 1843 by John Dillwyn Llewelyn at Penllergare, W. Glamorgan (From* The Gardeners Magazine, *1876).*

# The Triumph of Art over Nature: Victorian Gardens

The Victorian garden authority, Shirley Hibberd, said in *Rustic Adornments for Homes of Taste* (1857) that 'a garden is an artificial contrivance', a statement which reflects the general Victorian attitude to gardens. The architect of a house was often involved in the design of the gardens, and the most common style was Gothic or Tudor. Gothic could be said to have run amuck at Gwrych Castle (Clwyd), completed in about 1822 for Lloyd Bamford Hesketh. Described as 'pure romantic scenery', not only is the mansion turreted and crenellated, but so are the walls of the gardens and park. On a much more intimate scale is Machen House (Gwent), presented by Sir Charles Morgan of Tredegar House to his third son, the Reverend Charles Augustus Morgan, in 1831. In the succeeding four years the earlier house was enlarged to a handsome rectory and a garden was made, surrounded by a crenellated wall with mock turrets at intervals. Within, the layout was almost rococo, with winding paths, naturalistic ponds, a rockwork cascade, a small summerhouse and several cast iron fountains. The pond nearest the house was planned as a 'willow-pattern' garden, with a 'Chinese' stone bridge, a weeping willow next to it (replaced in the 1950s) and banks of rhododendrons.

Terraces made a reappearance around the house, and they are one of the most enduring features of nineteenth-century gardens. Good examples can be seen at Margam Castle, Golden Grove, Stradey Castle (Dyfed), Vaynor Park (Powys), Plas Tan-y-bwlch (Gwynedd), Leighton Hall, The Hendre, Hafodunos (Clwyd), Bryntysilio (Clwyd) and Kinmel Park. A crenellated terrace is all that remains of the huge 1850s house of Lawrenny Castle (Dyfed). Terraces were added to older houses, such as St Fagan's Castle (S. Glamorgan) and Dinefwr, and around eighteenth-century garden buildings such as the Margam orangery. At Baron Hill the house lies derelict and its magnificent terraces are abandoned and overgrown. In 1836-37 T. H. Wyatt rebuilt Llantarnam Abbey (Gwent), an earlier house which began life as a real Cistercian abbey, in Elizabethan Gothic for Reginald Blewitt. The garden terrace is surrounded with a castellated wall with corner bastions, and the park and forecourt are entered under Tudor archways.

Older formal features, such as the long approach avenue of limes at Soughton Hall, were allowed to remain. Gardens were laid out formally, often in pseudo-historical styles, which by the 1840s had crystallized into 'seventeenth-century parterre' or 'Italian Renaissance'. Fountains, statues, and other garden ornaments, often made of cast iron, artificial stone or terracotta, came back into fashion, as did the more artificial forms of planting such as topiary. The topiary yews and hedges on the east terrace at Chirk Castle were planted after 1872 by Richard Myddelton Biddulph. The parterre at Erddig, laid out with L-shaped beds, box, and rockwork fountains in 1861 by Blashfield's of Grantham, a prominent firm of landscape gardeners, gives a good idea of Victorian garden layout.

*The Victorian parterre at Erddig, Clwyd, with a rockwork fountain in the foreground. Laid out in 1861, it is a good example of garden layouts of the period (By courtesy of the Wales Tourist Board).*

The ha-ha went out of fashion after the 1820s, and the boundary between garden and park was usually a terrace wall or ornamental iron fencing. Formal features such as steps, avenues and cascades might lead the artificiality on out into the park. Nowhere is this more apparent than at Glynllifon, which was remodelled, probably by Edward Haycock, in a heavy Palladian style for Lord Newborough in 1836. Perhaps in memory of his late Italian wife, Lord Newborough laid out the garden in grand 'Italian Renaissance' style, with three big fountains set formally in line, down an avenue terminated by a long cascade. Some of the layout survives, including less formal features such as a children's boathouse and a miniature mill (built as a folly) with a grotto beneath it.

*The Victorian park surrounding Margam Castle, W. Glamorgan, where everything was planned on a grand scale in the 1830s (By courtesy of the Wales Tourist Board).*

In the 1830s the vast picturesque Margam Castle was designed in Tudor style by Thomas Hopper for the young Christopher Rice Mansel Talbot. Everything was done on a grand scale. In the grounds new carriage drives were made, lodges built (some in the 1840s by the architect Edward Haycock) and the ground around the house was levelled for terracing. The terraces were surrounded by elaborate balustrading and screens, and a series of huge steps was made down to the older orangery (see pp. 36-7) and remains of the medieval abbey, now, ironically, considered romantic. In order to make a large new kitchen and fruit garden to the west, the old village of Margam was demolished and the occupants housed in a new picturesque settlement called Groes – demolished in this century to make way for the M4 motorway. Much planting was done, and the fruit and vegetables of Margam quickly became famous.

The gardens of Leighton Hall in their heyday must have exhibited all the Victorian confidence and exuberance that were present in the greater gardens of the time. Leighton was primarily a model agricultural estate on a scale hardly seen before or after. It was built for a Liverpool banker, John Naylor, in the 1850s, with grand house, estate church, and numerous farm buildings designed by the Liverpool architect W. H. Gee in 'semi-Gothic' style. Technological innovation in the form of mechanization was used to the full for agricultural purposes, but was also turned to pleasurable ones: on Moel-y-Mab, the hilltop above the house, a black-and-white summerhouse was built, which could be reached by an inclined railway. The extensive gardens, now derelict, were designed in about 1860 by Edward Kemp, a pupil of Joseph Paxton, who a few years earlier had designed the gardens at Maesmawr Hall, Welshpool (Powys). Those at Leighton included a rose garden, a geometrical garden, and informal gardens with pools, cascades and raised walkways, and were adorned with carvings and statues, including a large lead one of Icarus on the point of falling from the skies into a pond.

At The Hendre the bones of a complete Victorian garden survive, at the core of the park already described (see p. 65). Made for the Rolls family after about 1830, it has balustraded terracing, garden pavilions, topiary (overgrown), a small sunk flower garden with a large cast-iron fountain in the middle, a long avenue, formerly of Lawson's cypresses, and an arboretum.

The stretch of Anglesey between Beaumaris and the Menai Bridge has been called 'Millionaire's Mile'. In the early nineteenth century Lord Bulkeley of Baron Hill built a new road to Beaumaris from the new Menai Bridge, and soon after several new mansions went up between it and the sea, including Craig-y-don, Rhianfa, Glan Menai and Glyn Garth (demolished). Rhianfa, a French Renaissance chateau designed by Charles Verelst of Liverpool, became celebrated for its hanging terraces, built in 1850-51 for two daughters of Sir John Hay Williams of Bodelwyddan Castle. Plants grew unchecked, and were encouraged to obscure and soften the architecture. The gardens of Rhianfa (now flats) became a model for the 'wild garden' of William Robinson later in the century (see p. 73).

# Eminent Victorian Garden Designs in Wales

As in earlier periods, some garden designers were widely admired and worked all over the country, including Wales. One such was the architect W. E. Nesfield, who specialized in formal gardens of elaborate parterres, two of which have survived in Wales. Nesfield altered Bodrhyddan (Clwyd) in 1873-74 for Conwy Rowley-Conwy, moving the main entrance from the south to the west side, building a new long drive, and designing the clipped yew walks and fine 'Dutch' baroque parterre in intricate patterns of box that is still in place on the south side. In 1871-74 Nesfield rebuilt Kinmel Park, the third rebuilding in a hundred years, for a descendant of the Reverend Edward Hughes, who had made a fortune extracting copper from the Parys mountain on Anglesey. The great red brick house in French chateau style was immensely grand, and to complement it Nesfield designed an equally grand terrace in 1873, in 'Venetian' style, with a grid layout, topiary and central fountain. This, plus a woodland garden on the slope above the house, was planted by Nesfield's

*The fine 'Dutch' baroque parterre at Bodrhyddan, Clwyd, the work of W. E. Nesfield in 1873-74 (Photograph: author).*

father, W. A. Nesfield, who also laid out the garden of the home farm of Kinmel in the 1860s.

The eminent Victorian garden designer Edward Milner (1819- 84), a protégé of Sir Joseph Paxton who worked with him on the gardens of the Crystal Palace in the 1850s, did a limited amount of work in Wales. His gardens usually had a formal terrace by the house, with pleasure grounds of lawns, flowing paths, specimen trees and shrubberies beyond. In the north he laid out the gardens of Bryn-y-Neuadd, Llanfairfechan (Gwynedd), in about 1858, and although the house has gone the bones of his garden, including a cast iron fountain, survive. He also worked on the gardens of Bodnant (see p. 74) in the 1870s, and produced plans for some work at Kinmel Park in 1883. In the south he designed the garden of Dingestow Court (Gwent), in 1883, and here the general outlines of his garden survive more or less intact, including a wide terrace in front of the house, and the unusual feature of a balloon-shaped fruit garden.

*An aerial view of Penrhyn Castle, Gwynedd, showing the Victorian walled garden in the bottom left (By courtesy of the Wales Tourist Board).*

# Planting in Victorian Gardens

**B**rightly coloured half-hardy exotic annuals are the hallmark of the Victorian garden. They were planted out in their thousands in flowerbeds of every conceivable shape and size, and Welsh gardens were no exception. However, their ephemeral nature means that only the names, often now completely strange-sounding and unfamiliar, have survived in the records of how these gardens looked. Trees and shrubs are more enduring, and exotic and even sub-tropical specimens became available and popular in the Victorian period.

From the beginning of the century rhododendrons were introduced to Britain, and quickly became popular in Wales, where they flourished in sheltered locations. Their main use was as underplanting in woodland, but they were also planted as specimen shrubs in gardens. A very early *Rhododendron ponticum,* brought over as a seedling from New York, was planted in 1800 in the garden of Tŷ Uchaf, the older house at Llanover Park. By the end of the century it was more than 160 feet (49m) in diameter. There were some specialist rhododendron gardens. One such is the late nineteenth-century garden of Blackaldern (Dyfed), planted by William Allen, an assiduous traveller and collector of plants in Tibet and other countries. Now the garden is a virtual forest of rhododendrons of all kinds, making a glorious spectacle in early summer. Stackpole Court was renowned not only for its extensive hot-houses but for the tender plants that grew outside in the

gardens. Swansea Bay, with luxuriant gardens like that of Clyne Castle, was another area where Victorian planting flourished.

Gwynedd came into its own as a region where Victorian gardens of conifers, rhododendrons, and exotic, even sub-tropical plants flourished. This was made possible on the one hand by the mild maritime climate of its coastal areas, especially where sheltered from the wind, and on the other by improved communications. The opening of Thomas Telford's road to Holyhead in 1819, and later the railways, enabled wealthy industrialists and others to establish homes and gardens in this beautiful countryside. Gwynedd was now within easy reach of businesses in north-west England and the Midlands. The most famous garden to take advantage of the benign climate was Bodnant (pp. 73-4). The gardens of Penrhyn Castle were particularly praised by nineteenth-century visitors, not just because of the magnificent situation, but because of the planting. Penrhyn Castle was a vast and serious essay in Gothic, designed for George Pennant by Thomas Hopper. Pennant's wealth came from West Indian possessions and the nearby slate quarries. Pennant's was the second 'castle' on the site in 30 years. Unusually, there were no surrounding terraces, but rather sloping lawns, as if recalling the style of Capability Brown. But further away all was Victorian. In a small walled garden, which still exists, formal beds contained luxuriant planting, including tender plants such as Chusan palms. The woodland, or wild garden was underplanted with many rare and tender shrubs. The long winding drive was edged with native bulbs and ferns, and the park was planted with fine trees. An unusual and much praised feature was a tunnel arbour of fuchsias. In 1859 Queen Victoria planted a Turkey oak and a wellingtonia (which survives) and Prince Arthur planted an English oak.

# Hot-Houses and the Productive Garden

The introduction in the late 1810s of hot-water heating systems, and the invention soon afterwards of the curved metal glazing bar, led to the huge success and popularity of hot-houses in the nineteenth century. The ability to grow a vast range of plants, including half-hardy annuals, tropical plants, ferns, orchids, vines, pineapples, and peaches in artificial climates under glass was a necessary adjunct to the grand Victorian life-style of endless entertaining, exotic food and decoration, and the massive bedding-out schemes. It was the head gardener's awesome responsibility to provide the necessary plants and cut flowers. Coomber of The Hendre, Cook of Brynkinalt, Forsyth of Hawarden Castle, Kent and Muir of Margam Castle, Mountford of Kinmel Park, Forder of Ruthin Castle (Clwyd), Speed of Penrhyn Castle, Harris of Singleton Abbey, Ewing of Bodorgan (Gwynedd) and Gough of Baron Hill were such men; skilled horticulturalists overseeing their vast domains of gardens, park and glass. Seeds and plants were obtained from nurseries all over Britain, but by about 1830 most major towns in Wales had nurserymen and seedsmen.

At Brynkinalt in the 1870s there were elaborate and extensive gardens, some of which had been laid out in 1808 by the duke of Wellington's grandmother, Charlotte viscountess Dungannon. Scroll, circular and shamrock-shaped beds (Victorian flowerbeds took almost any shape, and one commentator in 1839 complained that 'unmeaning flower beds in the shape of kidneys and tadpoles and sausages and leeches and commas now disfigure the lawn'), and two long ribbon borders were supplied with 90,000 bedding plants from the hot-houses each year. In 1873, at Baron Hill, 24,000 bedding plants were required to fill about twenty acres (8ha) of 'dressed ground' in the main garden and the separate garden of Nant. Thirty potted plants were changed every second day in the drawing room and hall, and more were needed for the conservatory, veranda and rest of the house, while Sir Richard Bulkeley also required a cucumber on the table every day of the year. Every grand mansion in the country had similar requirements, and it was a saying that the hot-houses of Tredegar House and Margam Castle could heat the world! At Bodorgan, on Anglesey, the gardener Mr Ewing invented and built unusual tall double glass walls between which peaches and apricots were grown. They were much commented on by visitors, and Ewing patented his design.

*An early nineteenth-century painting of Nerquis Hall, Clwyd, with Gothic greenhouse and vegetable beds. Hot-houses were popular in the Victorian period (By courtesy of Clwyd County Record Office).*

The great challenge was to produce pineapples all the year round – no small task seeing that it took two years to bring one to maturity. In 1878 the 'pines' of Singleton Abbey were boasted of as being the best in Wales. Those at Cyfarthfa Castle were also famous, and in the 1870s the head gardener claimed that he cut one a day each year, and 100 on each Christmas Day. Stackpole Court, The Hendre, and Penrhyn Castle were also noted for their pineapples.

Glasshouses are one of the least durable of garden structures, and when, after the First World War, there were no longer the resources or manpower to keep them going most were abandoned and left to rot. Very few survive. Some remain at Margam Castle, and there are fine conservatories at Penpont and Pantygoitre (Gwent). The kitchen garden at The Hendre retains its vinery and Black Hamburg vines, but most of the extensive ranges, including pineapple, peach, melon, strawberry, tomato, rose, carnation, fern, and orchid houses, have gone. Here nothing was done by halves, and it was possible to water plants with hot water from a huge underground tank, which still exists. Perhaps the saddest Welsh loss is the pioneering orchid house built in 1843 by John Dillwyn Llewellyn at Penllergare. It was an epiphyte house for non-terrestrial orchids. In it he attempted to create a tropical landscape, based on the Essequibo rapids, where one of the orchids he wanted to grow, *Huntleya violacea,* had been discovered. Above a central pool hot water splashed down a series of rocky ledges, creating a hot, steamy atmosphere. The orchids flourished and visitors were amazed by their 'wild luxuriance'. Now all that remains is an untidy and overgrown jumble of stone. Thirty years later an orchid house was a standard element in the grander garden.

From 1878 to 1919, the famous opera singer, Adelina Patti, lived at Craig-y-nos Castle (Powys), built in the remote upper Tawe valley in about 1842, and later much extended by her. She spent much time in her fine gardens, which included a huge rockery, a rose garden, two lakes, and the interlinked Winter Garden (a large iron-framed conservatory filled with tropical plants – subsequently moved to Swansea where it now forms the Patti Pavilion), aviary and another conservatory.

An interesting postscript to the story of Victorian glasshouses in Wales is the Wardian case, a sealed miniature conservatory invented in the 1840s by Dr Nathaniel Bagshaw Ward. The frontispiece of the second edition of Ward's book on the subject (1852), and a popular model, was the 'Tintern-Abbey Case', so-called because it contained 'a small model, built in pumice and Bath stone, of the west window of Tintern Abbey'. The invention was to prove immensely popular, and was much used for transporting plants around the world.

## Victorian Grottoes

There were other, more incidental elements in the nineteenth-century garden, and relics of some of them survive. In the early nineteenth century the Gothic novel was popular, with its macabre scenes, haunted graveyards, headless knights and clanking chains. In the garden, a dark and gloomy grotto could produce a satisfying frisson of fear. The best grotto of this kind in Wales is at Talacre Abbey (Clwyd). The mansion was built in Gothic style for the Mostyn family on the site of an earlier one in 1824-29, and the grotto probably dates

from soon afterwards. It stands next to an equally fantastic folly tower on the hill above the house, and looks from the outside like an irregular heap of stones, whose water-worn appearance is achieved by a coating of mortar. Inside, the grotto's labyrinthine form becomes apparent, with twisting passages, dark chambers, steps and openings, all built of mortar-covered stone, and encrusted with shells, coloured stones and stalactites. It soon becomes apparent that the intention was agreeably to frighten the visitor: built into the entrance is a monster, so contrived that it could 'breathe fire' (by lighting a fire behind it); further on a ghoulish 'ghost' is fashioned on a wall; and in the innermost recess is a life-sized figure of a headless monk.

*A ghostly presence in the grotto at Talacre, Clwyd. The grotto is the best example of its kind in Wales (Photograph: author).*

It is said that Mostyn children brought new governesses there to test their mettle. The tower, a sham Gothic ruin, is of the same rocky construction, with patterns of stones and shells embedded in the vaulted ceiling of the lower floor. The gardens immediately around the house are also embellished with the same rockwork.

There are fragments of similar 'Gothic' structures elsewhere in Wales, including a life-sized figure of a kneeling monk that is all that is left of the grotto at Llantarnam Abbey. Other kinds of grottoes continued to be fashionable, and later in the Victorian period coalesced with rockeries and ferneries.

*This 'Gothic' figure of a kneeling monk is all that remains of the Victorian grotto at Llantarnam Abbey.*

# The Rustic and Picturesque

**D**espite the disapproval of J.C. Loudon, a liking for the rustic continued undiminished in the nineteenth century. Garden buildings of roots, moss, tree trunks, and bark were by their very nature ephemeral, and few remain in Wales. However, it is known that there were roothouses at Emral Hall (Clwyd), and a rustic summerhouse survives at Penpont. At the foot of the Wyndcliffe a moss house – a rustic building with a thatched roof covered in moss, and Gothic windows with stained glass – was built in 1828 by the duke of Beaufort's steward, Osmond Wyatt, next to the new road from Chepstow to Tintern. Above it he made the 365 Steps up to the top of the cliff, where a viewing platform, the 'Eagle's Nest' was built. The moss house became popular with tourists, who were given an hour to take tea there by the Chepstow coachman. If they felt energetic they could climb the 365 Steps to admire the view from the top. They then moved on to Tintern, where they were allowed two hours.

A magnificent survivor in the rustic style is the shell hermitage at Pontypool Park, which stands at the very top of the park. It was built in the 1830s for Capel Hanbury Leigh to a design of the Bath architect, S. G. Tit. It is said to have been the inspiration of Hanbury Leigh's first wife, Molly Mackworth. The outside is a plain circular stone building with a conical roof, giving no hint of the riot of rustic fancy within. The floor is set with bones and teeth forming patterns of interlacing arcs, stars and a ring of hearts and diamonds. The vaulted ceiling is held on slender pillars encrusted with rocks and shells, with different patterns on each pillar. On the ceiling are stalactites – some false, some real – and shells, spar, and crystals, in delicate patterns. Branches, elm bosses, ivy stems, lumps of bark, and dried moss decorate the walls. The windows, now plain, originally held stained glass, and miraculously five of the original six rustic chairs remain. The Hanbury family had picnics here, lighting a fire in the fireplace, and bringing fresh moss to arrange in the crevices in the walls. In the American Gardens at the north end of the park is the slightly earlier Rustic Lodge, a small picturesque building built of boulders. There is a contemporary shell hermitage at Cilwendig (Dyfed), with similar decoration of knucklebone mosaic floors, shells in the walls and quartz rocks imitating flames on the gables.

The rustic in the garden was also manifested in elaborate arrangements of rockwork, sometimes of real stone, sometimes artificial. In the mid century

Left: The plain exterior of the shell hermitage in Pontypool Park belies the magnificent rustic decoration inside. It was built in the 1830s.

Below: A detail of the internal shellwork at Pontypool Park (Photographs: author).

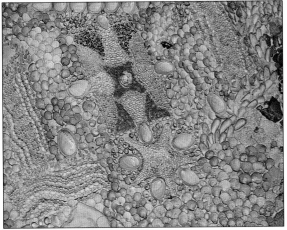

Pulhamite stone (see p. 65) was popular, and some realistic rock faces and cascades were made of it in Wales, for instance at The Hendre. Bedwellty Park, built in the early nineteenth century for the ironmaster Samuel Homfray and his son, is embellished with much rockwork. As well as lining paths and flowerbeds, and covering the banks between a series of pools, there is a whole area of the gardens devoted especially to it. A path with large water-worn rocks set upright next to it leads under a rustic arch of similar stones to a paved garden with a series of linked circular openings, one with a rockwork fountain in the middle, and all surrounded with rockwork. Elsewhere in the park are further contemporary features, including a now collapsing rustic stone pavilion and a well preserved ice-house, topped most unexpectedly by a belfry.

Rare survivals are the mounds on which some of the park trees were planted, a fashion introduced by J. C. Loudon which became popular in the middle of the century.

# Castle and Abbey Gardens

Real ruins were still considered picturesque ornaments in the landscape or garden in the Victorian period, for example at Hawarden Castle. Those already famous, such as Chepstow Castle and Tintern Abbey, continued to be much visited. Some were treated more or less as picturesque gardens, and were adorned with lawns, flowerbeds, rustic seats and tables. One such was Raglan Castle, laid out for the duke of Beaufort by his steward, Osmond Wyatt, in about 1830. Serious thought was given to the visual appearance of ruins, with publications such as William Robinson's *Alpine Flowers for the Garden* (1870), which had a section on 'Ruin and wall gardens'. Climbing plants were advocated, and ivy, thought to enhance romantic appeal, was allowed to smother the walls. In the last quarter of the nineteenth century William Nevill, fifth earl and first marquis of Abergavenny, laid out Abergavenny Castle as a 'place of recreation' for the general public, with winding paths and circular flowerbeds. But the crowning glory of the gardens was the riot of rustic woodwork on the castle walls, with wall-walks, gazebos, fences, and arbours covering every available surface.

Private gardens were also made around castles, ruined or inhabited. At Ruthin Castle there were flourishing formal Victorian gardens within the old castle walls, made to complement the new castle initially built in 1826 for Frederick West, and later enlarged in 1848-53 for his son. A visitor in 1891 was struck by the contrast between the old castle 'where instruments of war and torture once glittered in defiant hands' and the garden where 'the more noble instruments of tillage are now brandished in the arts of peace'. A house was constructed in the ruins of Newport Castle (Dyfed), in 1859, for its owner Thomas Lloyd, and the moat below was turned into a pleasure ground, with walks and a boating pond. Towards the end of the nineteenth century J. R. Cobb, a wealthy antiquary, bought and restored Pembroke, Manorbier and Caldicot Castles. He made his home at the latter, laying out the inner ward as a garden, and planting many trees in the surrounding park.

At Cardiff Castle the third marquis of Bute and his architect William Burges began work on transforming the castle in 1868. Work began on the gardens in 1871, with an informal landscape within the walls, and a modified Burges garden in the moat on the south side, comprising a sloping lawn and large circular beds. Both were laid out by the head gardener, Andrew Pettigrew. One of the more bizarre ventures of the third marquis was the planting in 1875 of a huge vineyard of Gamay Noir grapes on the slopes below Castell Coch. In the long term the experiment was not a success, and by 1914 the family had admitted defeat. But in the 1890s the wines were placed on the London market, listed as 'Welsh Wines; Canary Brand', described rather enigmatically as 'eminently wholesome and honest'.

# Public Parks and Cemeteries

Philip Yorke of Erddig was somewhat ahead of his time in opening his park to the public in 1779 (see p. 6). Although some owners allowed visitors into their private parks in the eighteenth century, it was usually under a carefully regulated system, as for instance at Hafod and Piercefield. But in the nineteenth century the dramatic increase in the urban population of Wales led to the idea of urban parks for public recreation, and this movement gathered momentum from the middle of the century onwards.

The parks were laid out with walks, conifers, and much colourful bedding, often in mounded beds. Bandstands and conservatories were added, and later, sports facilities. In 1854 the marchioness of Bute began laying out the Sophia Gardens to the west of the River Taff in Cardiff, and in 1858 the public was granted access, making them perhaps the earliest urban public park in Wales. Another early park was the small Rock Park in the spa town of Llandrindod Wells (Powys), landscaped with paths and much conifer planting in the 1860s. Others followed, including the Victoria Gardens in Neath, Aberdare Park (Mid Glamorgan), laid out by William Barron of Sketty, Swansea, in the 1870s, and Roath Park in Cardiff, created in 1887, which originally had an extensive botanical garden.

Landscaped public cemeteries were a related development, linked to the great growth of urban population, and to the periodic outbreaks of fatal diseases such as cholera. Many were established in the 1850s, and later laid out in high Victorian fashion by firms of nurserymen with winding drives and paths, and much evergreen planting. The new Carmarthen cemetery (Dyfed), St Woolos Cemetery, Newport (Gwent), and the New Cemetery, Abergavenny (Gwent) are good examples.

# Chapter 7
# The Edwardian Era and Beyond

*The Canal Terrace and Pin Mill at Bodnant, Gwynedd. The naturalistic garden at Bodnant is one of the best examples of this kind in Britain (National Trust Photographic Library/Ian Shaw).*

## Transitions

The late Victorian period was one of transition, which in style and outlook foreshadowed the Edwardian era, from 1901 to 1914. This whole period, from about 1880 to 1914, was in many ways a golden age of gardens in Britain. The earlier confidence of the Victorian period remained, with owners of estates and large-scale gardens still able to afford the staff to maintain them. However, times were getting harder, servant numbers had to be curtailed, and gardens, therefore, had to become less labour-intensive and costly to run. It was also a time when the rigid hierarchies of Victorian society were being broken down in favour of greater informality, and this was also reflected in gardens.

Various styles of gardens emerged, such as the naturalistic garden advocated by William Robinson (the eminent garden writer), the Arts-and-Crafts garden, the architectural garden promoted by architects such as Edwin Lutyens, softened by the lush planting of the famous gardener and garden designer Gertrude Jekyll, and the Italianate garden of architects such as T. H. Mawson. A few fine gardens of all these types were made in Wales.

Most were commissioned by wealthy industrialists, colliery owners and professional men. The character of gardens was influenced by the flood of new plant introductions, and there was also a move away from gaudy bedding (which was very costly to produce) and artificiality towards a greater use of perennials and softer colours.

## The Naturalistic Garden

The most famous garden of this kind in Wales, and one of the best in Britain, is Bodnant. Henry Pochin, an industrial chemist and conifer enthusiast from Lancashire, saw the possibilities of the rocky gorge of the River Hiraethlyn, a tributary of the Conwy, and bought the estate, then called Bodnod, in 1874. The situation was a romantic one, with views westwards to the Snowdon range. Pochin planted the gorge, which became known as the Dell, with a wide range of conifers, which have now grown to giant proportions. After 1909 his grandson, Henry Duncan McLaren (1879-1953), who became the second Lord Aberconway, planted many rhododendrons, the most important of which were early Chinese introductions of the plant-hunters E. H. Wilson, Frank Kingdon-Ward, J. F. Rock, and

George Forrest. Further underplantings of moisture-loving plants turned the Dell into the kind of wild garden advocated by William Robinson. Meanwhile, above the Dell, the slope up to the house was transformed between 1904 and 1914 into a series of terraces. Initially, in the 1870s, Edward Milner had laid out the slope with formal beds and shrubberies. Now the second Lord Aberconway made the five Italianate terraces that still exist today, the Upper Rose Terrace, the Croquet Lawn, the Lily Terrace, the Lower Rose Garden, and the Canal Terrace, positioned so as to avoid disturbing his grandfather's magnificent cedars. The Canal Terrace is probably the best known. At one end stands the Pin Mill (built in about 1730 as a summerhouse at Woodchester, Gloucestershire, then used as a pin factory, and moved to Bodnant in 1939) and at the other end is an Italianate yew theatre. The list of rare and beautiful plants at Bodnant is endless, and their flourishing condition is in part due to the benign climate, and in part to the skilled horticultural partnership between the Aberconway family and their head gardeners, who since 1920 have been F. C. Puddle, his son Charles, and his grandson Martin. Since 1949 the National Trust has entered this partnership, and Bodnant has remained one of the gardening wonders of Britain.

*Part of the Japanese garden at Shirenewton Hall, Gwent, created in the early 1900s (Photograph: author).*

The Japanese garden was an offshoot of the naturalistic garden, albeit a rather esoteric one. At the turn of the century, as Japan was slowly opened up to the West, Japanese gardens, although their underlying philosophy and symbolism were little understood, became very fashionable. Miniature versions of gardens in Japan, such as that of the Katsura imperial villa in Kyoto, sprang up here and there all over Britain, complete with rock-edged naturalistic lakes or pools, islands, bridges, water basins, wells, cascades, stone lanterns, pagodas, sculptured tortoises, cranes, tea pavilions, and Japanese planting such as bamboos,

*The terraces at Bodnant, Gwynedd, created by the second Lord Aberconway between 1904 and 1914 (By courtesy of the Wales Tourist Board).*

pines, maples, ferns and mosses. A few were made in Wales. Bodrhyddan, for example, had a 'path of life' garden, and at Plas Dinam (Powys) – built for Captain J. O. Crewe-Read by W. E. Nesfield in 1873-4 – there was a 'Japanese wood'. There was also a Japanese garden at Llantilio Court, the bones of which – a pool and island reached by an arched bridge, now reduced to its iron framework – remain. Bamboos became popular, and bamboo gardens were planted at The Hendre and Margam Castle.

But the best preserved Welsh Japanese garden is at Shirenewton Hall (Gwent). It was made in the early years of the present century by Charles Liddell, a wealthy shipper in the Far Eastern trade. The structures were imported from Japan, twisted maples and pines abound, and the layout is so cunning that an illusion of space is given even though the garden cannot be more than an acre in size. Around every corner there is a new vista, another pond, a cascade, another bridge, a stone lantern, a pagoda, a well, a stone mushroom, and yet everything is hidden. It is indeed true to the spirit of the Japanese garden.

# The Architectural, Arts-and-Crafts, and Italianate Garden

These three types of garden shared a common creative aim, albeit with slightly different emphases. The unifying idea was to reflect the architecture of the house in the garden. Thus the English vernacular style, which became very popular, taking its cue from houses and gardens of old Jacobean England, led to renewed interest in topiary, and 'old' flowers were sought. The fine Edwardian garden at Gwydir (Gwynedd) included a topiary garden called the 'Old Dutch Garden'. At Bodysgallen (Gwynedd) a rose garden and sunken 'Dutch' garden were made south of the house by Lady Douglas Pennant on her marriage in 1888 to Colonel Henry Mostyn. The entire terraced gardens, older though they seem, date from this period. The architect, F. Inigo Thomas, remodelled the Nash house of Ffynone (Dyfed) for John Colby in 1904. Below it he proposed an elaborate scheme of terraces rather like those of Powis Castle, but only the top terrace, with a semi-circular grotto at the east end, was built. The mid nineteenth-century formal terraced gardens at St Fagan's Castle were added to in the Edwardian period by Viscount Windsor and his head gardener Hugh Pettigrew, son of the marquis of Bute's head gardener. As well as vast new kitchen gardens, situated where the

Folk Museum now stands, were a Thyme Garden and an Italian Garden.

Much of the present appearance of the terraced gardens at St Donat's Castle is due to the alterations of the owner, Morgan Stuart Williams, at the beginning of the twentieth century. On the Tudor terraces he added a formal 'Tudor' garden, with 'Queen's beasts' on octagonal stone columns, an Italianate summerhouse, and a loggia. In the 1920s the sixth marquis of Anglesey created a formal terraced Italianate rose garden at Plas Newydd. An Edwardian conservatory had stood on the upper terrace, but the lower terraces replaced sloping lawns and Victorian flowerbeds.

*The Italianate terraced garden at Plas Newydd, Anglesey, created in the 1920s (National Trust Photographic Library/Martin Trelawny).*

The architect, T. H. Mawson, worked more in the Italianate style, and had several commissions in Wales. One of the earliest was in 1891-92 at Wern, near Portmadoc (Gwynedd), where he created an entirely new terraced garden for the slate quarry owner, Richard Greaves. The structure of it survives as the grounds of a nursing home. In 1898-99 he designed a large hillside garden, which included the new idea of a herb garden, at The Flagstaff, Colwyn Bay (Clwyd), for the surgeon, Dr Walter Whitehead. It is now the Welsh Mountain Zoo, and little remains. Other commissions included Beechwood Park, Newport (Gwent), which in 1900 became a public park, Cefnfaes Hall (Powys), and Bodelwyddan Castle, where he carried out some 'necessary improvements' in 1910, including the pillared entrance to the walled garden. In 1893 he designed a public park in Newport (Gwent, see p. 78).

But Mawson's most lasting memorial in Wales is the garden at Dyffryn (S. Glamorgan), designed in 1906 in collaboration with the owner, Reginald Cory, a dedicated amateur horticulturalist and 'keen draughtsman'. The garden was begun in 1893 for Reginald's father, to complement his big new house. Mawson expanded the Victorian garden to the south, laying out a huge lawn, axial canal and lily pond in the middle of which is a magnificent dragon fountain. He linked the much earlier walled garden west of the house to this formal area with a series of enclosures in which 'we felt at liberty to

The canal and fountain at Dyffryn, S. Glamorgan, created at the beginning of the twentieth century by T. H. Mawson (By courtesy of the Wales Tourist Board).

indulge in every phase of garden design which the site and my client's catholic views suggested'. Thus there is a Japanese room, a Pompeiian room, and a cloistered room, as well as other specialized gardens. Cory keenly supported plant-hunters such as Wilson, Forrest and Farrer, and many of the trees at Dyffryn are early introductions. Parts of the scheme, such as the 'roof garden' over the colonnade, have gone, and other parts, like the naturalistic lake, never worked, but overall the gardens are one of the best preserved of the period in Wales.

Glan y Mawddach is an architectural garden of formal terraces in a spectacular position overlooking the Mawddach estuary. It was laid out at the

beginning of the twentieth century by a Mrs Keithley, whose family emblem, the griffon, appears all over the garden. Balustrades, urns and clipped hedges give it an Italianate feel, but the planting is luxuriant, and above the house is an informally laid out Japanese garden. At the very top of the garden is a 'castle garden' of curving terraces in a clearing in the wood, overlooking a small ruined tower.

In 1913-15 the Arts-and-Crafts architect, C. E. Mallows, designed a house and garden at Craig-y-parc, Pentyrch (M. Glamorgan), for a colliery owner, Thomas Evans. The garden, which still exists, is formal and terraced on one side and a wilder woodland and water garden on the other.

High Glanau, Gwent: the last home in Wales of the writer and garden architect, Avray Tipping (Photograph: author).

Tucked away in the south-east corner of Wales, in Gwent, are four of the best Welsh gardens of this period, made by the writer and garden architect, H. Avray Tipping. Three – Mathern Palace, Mounton House, and High Glanau – were for himself, and one – Wyndcliffe Court – was for a friend. Tipping's gardens were divided into compartments bounded by yew hedging often sculpted into battlements or with topiary birds and animals on top, long grass bowling greens, wild areas, and lush planting within a formal framework. The structure and yew hedging of these gardens remain, even if the detail has been lost.

Mathern Palace was one of the chief residences of the bishops of Llandaff from the fifteenth century until about 1700. When Tipping bought it in 1894 it was reduced to 'the sordid untidiness of a hopelessly ill-contrived and unrepaired farmstead'. He sympathetically restored the palace and laid out a garden of terraces and compartments bounded by yew hedging, with a wilder rock garden down the slope on the north side, at the foot of which were the medieval fishponds. Most of this survives, including the massive yew arbour on the upper terrace and the Banksian roses on the walls. Tipping's next garden, Mounton House, was much more ambitious and architectural. In 1907 he bought land in the Mounton valley below it, and laid it out as a naturalistic garden, but in 1911, after inheriting a fortune, he bought land on the plateau above, and in collaboration with the architect, Eric Francis, built a large Arts-and-Crafts house with a long axial approach to the north, and terraced garden compartments with wild garden below to the south. At the east end of the terrace is a pergola of massive stone piers around a now empty pool, and to its east is a delightful half-timbered pavilion overlooking the croquet lawn.

Tipping's view that there should be architecture round the house with wood and wild gardens beyond was perfectly realized at High Glanau, which he built for himself between 1918 and 1923. The dramatic situation on the western edge of a high plateau, with spectacular views over Gwent, lent itself to his terraces, with a central axis of steps leading down to an octagonal lily pool. Below and to the side of this he made woodland gardens, with winding paths and glades, and planted them with a wide range of shade-loving plants. Tipping called the management of these woodlands 'gardening but with nature kept in the forefront'.

*Wyndcliffe Court, Gwent: Avray Tipping helped in the design of this terraced garden (Photograph: author).*

Wyndcliffe Court, an Arts-and-Crafts house high up above the Wye valley, was built for Charles Clay by Eric Francis, architect of Mounton House and High Glanau. Tipping had a hand in the design of the garden, which follows his now familiar pattern. The sloping site was cleverly levelled, and axes were created using steps and yew hedging. From a delightful summerhouse in the corner of a sunken pool garden there is a spectacular view out over the coastal plain to the Bristol Channel and beyond.

Percy Cane was a garden designer working in more or less the same idiom. He altered the historic

gardens at Llannerch in the late 1920s, and his layout of spacious Italianate terraced gardens, arched loggia, a long rose walk flanked by pergolas, and an informal woodland garden survives in part.

# *Plantsmens' Gardens*

Gardens whose character was largely determined by planting are beyond the scope of this book, but a few of the more important ones should be mentioned. The gardens of Chirk Castle owe their present-day appearance largely to twentieth-century planting by Algernon Myddleton Biddulph, Lady Howard de Walden, Norah Lindsay, and latterly the National Trust. From 1939 onwards the three Misses Keating restored and planted a Victorian garden overlooking the sea at Plas yn Rhiw on the Lleyn peninsula (Gwynedd). Their

*Compartments and exuberant planting at Plas yn Rhiw, Gwynedd (National Trust Photographic Library / Martin Trelawny).*

planting gave the formal garden a wild luxuriance, and many of their magnolias, rhododendrons, camellias and eucryphias survive. One of the finest twentieth-century collections of rhododendrons in Britain, recently rescued from neglect, was built up at Clyne Castle in Swansea in the 1920s and 1930s by Admiral Heneage-Vivian. Colby Wood Garden (now cared for by the National Trust), an informal woodland garden, was created early in the twentieth century by Miss E. F. D. Mason of Colby Lodge. The garden of the well-known plantsman and writer, A. T. Johnson, survives at Ro-wen (Gwynedd). Johnson specialized in labour-saving and ericaceous plants, and species roses, and made the garden between the first and second world wars.

Gwendoline Elizabeth and Margaret Davies planted on a lavish scale at Gregynog. Conifers, rhododendrons, and the golden yew hedge on the bank in front of the house were already well established when they took over in 1920, but in the next twenty years they added many new areas, including the dingle, which Avray Tipping helped to design, a pool garden, woodland gardens, and a bog garden called the Dell. The sisters were reluctant to thin, but the resulting wild luxuriance has now more or less disappeared. When the gardens were at their peak in 1939, 23 gardeners were employed, including a small permanent staff in the Dell.

*The golden yew hedge at Gregynog, Powys (By courtesy of the Wales Tourist Board).*

One of the strangest gardens in Wales, that at Dewstow House (Gwent), was created in the early years of the twentieth century by the owner Henry Oakley, for the growing of ferns. It is a labyrinthine underground garden! Winding passages lead to top-lit chambers with pools, fountains, cascades, artificial rockwork and stalactites, with beds and niches for the ferns which once flourished here. Oakley may well have been influenced in his fern

*One of the underground chambers at Dewstow House, Gwent. It represents one of the strangest gardens in Wales (Photograph: author).*

growing by his near neighbour, the renowned fern expert E. J. Lowe, who lived at Shirenewton Hall from about 1880 to 1900, and who grew an extensive collection of ferns. But there was nothing resembling Oakley's underground gardens at Shirenewton.

# Public Parks

Urban public parks continued to be created in the late Victorian and Edwardian eras. Between 1880 and 1890 Cathays Park in Cardiff was greatly enlarged by the marquis of Bute, giving the city the largest central parkland of any British city. The first marquis of Abergavenny laid out Abergavenny Castle as a public park (see p. 72). Some private parks became public ones, and their character changed with the addition of recreational amenities. Beechwood Park in Newport became public in 1900, Bedwellty Park in Tredegar in 1901, Pontypool Park in 1920, and Plas Machynlleth (Powys), in 1948.

In 1893 T. H. Mawson won a competition to design Bellevue Park in Newport (Gwent), but because of a clerical error his design was for the field next to that earmarked for the park. Luckily the mayor and corporation did not notice the discrepancy, and Mawson was able surreptitiously to alter his plans to suit the new site. The sloping ground was landscaped with winding paths, specimen trees and a rocky stream with cascades in the middle, similar to the one he designed for Beechwood Park. Later, in 1910, terraces, a tea pavilion and conservatories were added.

# 'Architect Errant': Clough Williams-Ellis

The architectural flight of fancy of Clough Williams-Ellis at Wales's most famous public park, Portmeirion, on the Glaslyn peninsula in north Wales (Gwynedd), is justly renowned. But perhaps less well known is the garden *tour de force* of this remarkable architect and early conservationist at Plas Brondanw nearby. Armed with the dramatic mountain backdrop of Snowdonia, and his dilapidated seventeenth-century family home, to which he was passionately attached, Clough Williams-Ellis slowly created one of Wales's most impressive gardens. From 1908 to 1914, and again after the First World War, he made a series of terraces, compartments and vistas delineated with now massive yew hedging. Each vista led the eye to one of the surrounding mountains – Moel Hebog, Moelwyn, Cnicht, and

Snowdon itself – which were thus drawn into the garden. Some axes terminated in features within the garden, like the raised roundel called the Apollo belvedere, and the orangery, built in 1914. One vista led the eye to his folly, Castell Brondanw, on a nearby hillside. The fire monument was erected in the garden by Williams-Ellis as a reminder that the house was completely gutted by fire in the winter of 1950-51, though he subsequently rebuilt it.

Portmeirion, begun in 1926, and not 'finished' until the 1970s, is pure theatre. In 1862 a mansion (converted to a hotel by Williams-Ellis) was built on the eastern end of the Penrhyn peninsula. Extensive woodland gardens known as the Gwyllt were planted on the end of the peninsula, and in them a famous collection of rhododendrons was established by Caiton Haig, breeder of the variety 'Gwyllt King'. On the drive is an earlier Victorian house, in Gothic style, now called Castell Deudraeth. Ironically the remains of the real castle had been razed in about 1869 'lest the ruins should become known and attract visitors to the place'.

*A portrait of Clough Williams-Ellis (By courtesy of The Hotel Portmeirion).*

Williams-Ellis embellished the Gwyllt woodlands with exotic plants, viewpoints, and 18 miles (29km) of walks. In the village itself flower gardens and shrubs, especially rhododendrons and hydrangeas, were planted to complement the eclectic range of architecture.

The gardens of Llangoed Castle (Powys) in the upper Wye valley, built by Williams-Ellis for Archibald Christy between 1913 and 1919, have fared less well, the house having been abandoned for 50 years before recent restoration as a hotel. But his last commission in Wales is in happier shape. Between 1956 and the early 1970s Williams-Ellis remodelled Nantclwyd Hall (Clwyd) for Sir Vivyan Naylor-Leyland. Ideas poured out (on paper), including temples, follies, a castellated duck-shooting platform and Palladian dog kennels. What was actually built was an elaborate garden with pavilions and gates that have been described as 'a cross between Cape Dutch and the sort of theatrical Italianate usually encountered only in sets for operas'. The park was embellished with bridges, a temple, a rotunda in eighteenth-century style, and a reservoir outfall built as a kind of grotto. Into this one estate Williams-Ellis managed to compress almost the whole of the history of parks and gardens in Wales.

*Clough Williams-Ellis's Portmeirion, begun in 1926, has become the most famous public park in Wales, and one of the best known in Britain (By courtesy of The Hotel Portmeirion).*

# Index of Places and People